the series on school reform

Patricia A. Wasley
University of Washington

Ann Lieberman
Carnegie Foundation for the
Advancement of Teaching

Joseph P. McDonald
New York University

SERIES EDITORS

the series on school reform, *continued*

SECOND EDITION

Looking Together at Student Work

Tina Blythe
David Allen
Barbara Schieffelin Powell

Teachers College, Columbia University
New York and London

Published by Teachers College Press, 1234 Amsterdam Avenue, New York, NY 10027

Library of Congress Cataloging-in-Publication Data

Blythe, Tina, 1964–
   Looking together at student work / Tina Blythe, David Allen, and Barbara
Schieffelin Powell ; new foreword by David N. Perkins. — 2nd ed.
       p.   cm. — (Series on school reform)
   Includes bibliographical references.
   ISBN 978-0-8077-4835-0 (pbk : alk. paper)
   1. Grading and marking (Students)—United States.   2. Educational tests and
measurements—United States.   I. Allen, David.   II. Powell, Barbara Schieffelin.
III. Title.

LB3051.B54 2008
371, 27—dc22
                                                                              2007024211

ISBN 978-0-8077-4835-0 (paper)

Printed on acid-free paper
Manufactured in the United States of America

15   14   13   12   11   10   09   08   8   7   6   5   4   3   2   1

Contents

 # Foreword

"Two heads are more numerous than one!" A number of years ago, someone mentioned to me this ironic twist on the traditional "two heads are better than one." I suppose I have remembered it ever since because it often seems the most that one can say. Our experiences of colloquy in family conversations, faculty meetings, and committee huddles commonly involve multiple heads without notably better thinking.

The uninspiring baseline of everyday experience makes me especially excited about this probing and practical guide from Tina Blythe, David Allen, and Barbara Powell. They give us cause for confidence that professional educators can put their heads together to good effect.

One clear message is the value of a nimble balance between systematicity and flexibility. System is essential to make these complex conversations focused and generative. Without protocols to guide the art and craft, it is all too easy to flop around. Important dimensions are likely to get missed altogether in the shaggy chaos of unstructured conversation—for instance, the descriptive aspect of student work, in which teachers are encouraged to see what is there without heavy evaluation or interpretation.

On the flexibility side, protocols do not mean catechisms. The authors offer three carefully developed protocols that have seen extended use, but they refrain from any orthodoxy. This feature doesn't work for you? Modify, discard, import a new element! Additionally, the authors profile schools where educators rolled up their sleeves and assembled their own protocols to serve particular agendas.

I can testify personally to the value of teachers' looking at student work with protocols. Several colleagues and I have been working for some time on ways teachers can foster the development of thinking and thoughtful learning, an undertaking we call Visible Thinking. Some colleagues of mine assembled a protocol not very different from those discussed here to help teachers look for the thinking in student work. It has provided teachers with a potent means of both improving craft and fostering collegiality. We encouraged the formation of cross-grade and cross-disciplinary groups of teachers and were impressed by how the conversations nourished mutual understanding and respect.

A few years ago, I did some thinking and writing about what makes groups and organizations smart. It seemed to me that there were two important dimensions to a truly productive exchange: knowledge processing and symbolic conduct. Knowledge processing means the thoughtful handling of knowledge—reaching for evidence, examining alternative interpretations, thinking outside the box, and so on. The authors of *Looking Together at Student Work* explain how good protocols and good facilitation contribute to this.

However, the story isn't done with the achievement of technically better group thinking. Just as important is the symbolic conduct, the tacit messages shared with one another about respect, solidarity, critical reflectiveness, thoughtful disagreement, and more. In the many examples the authors provide, it's plain that building a strong collaborative culture is just as much the mission as advancing particular conversations.

So let me commend these practices of looking together at student work as powerful resources not just for the technical but for the cultural enterprise of education. Yes, two heads or three or eight are better than one—not just more numerous—provided we put our heads together in smart ways.

—David N. Perkins
Professor, Harvard Graduate School of Education

Foreword to
First Edition

ACROSS THE COUNTRY AND ABROAD, school reformers have recognized the pressing need to place actual student work formally and respectfully at the center of both public and private conversations about school. From California to Vermont, from school reform organizations to their many working partners in schools, teaching centers, and universities, people are trying out new tools for making change through that most radical of activities: unarmed discussion.

When people who come at school change with very different beliefs and assumptions meet to look at student work, their mutual understanding often deepens. Using diplomatic protocols that make communication feel "safe," they often find common ground and can move more surely toward creating the conditions in which teachers and students might do better throughout the system.

Although these tools differ, all share a focus on bringing together people across the school community—teachers, parents, students, and outside visitors—to look at student work. All aim to learn something that will then affect future teaching and learning, not just the individual student whose work they examine. And all provide a formal structure, or "protocol," that, while often uncomfortable at first, surfaces and values different points of view.

David Allen has compared such protocols to putting on a play, "though the dialogue," he notes, "is mainly improvisational." Yet just as theatrical styles that range from classical to "method" can all work magic on the mind and the soul, effective protocols have their styles and purposes too.

Some fall on the more evaluative end of the spectrum, aiming to analyze and thus improve teaching strategies and curriculum. Others rely more on close description to heighten teachers' understanding of individual children and hence affect teacher practice. Some look at a moment in time and extend its meaning outward; others take an accumulated body of evidence and draw new meanings from its larger picture.

Thoughtful, rigorous, and user friendly, this book lays out some of the best ways to go about this process. Any group of teachers, parents, or community members could use it to participate in the hard work of assessing where our schools are and how they can improve.

Once begun, that cycle of reflecting together on direct evidence, drawing out its meaning, and then folding what we learn back into the daily work may prove the very engine of school change in the critical years ahead. "I used to think student work was between student and teacher," one teacher told me recently. "Now I think all work should be as public, and as shared, as possible." When a teacher can say that, things have begun to move. This book will help.

—Kathleen Cushman
Cofounder, What Kids Can Do, Inc.

Preface

THE ORIGINAL VERSION OF THIS GUIDE was intended as a companion to *Assessing Student Learning: From Grading to Understanding* (Teachers College Press, 1998). This second edition expands on the goals of the first: to provide teachers and administrators with strategies and resources for working together to examine and discuss student work—science projects, essays, artwork, math problems, and more. To give some real examples of the ways teachers and administrators do this, we describe three protocols, or structures for conversations: the Collaborative Assessment Conference, the Tuning Protocol, and, new in this edition, the Consultancy. We also include three case studies from schools that developed their own protocols for looking at student work. We do not describe other valuable protocols such as the Descriptive Review processes, Primary Language Record, the Slice, or Standards in Practice. For more information about these, as well as the Collaborative Assessment Conference, the Tuning Protocol, and the Consultancy, see *Assessing Student Learning* and the materials included in the list of resources at the end of this volume.

A NOTE ABOUT TERMINOLOGY

The protocols we describe in this book are appropriate for teachers and administrators working at all grades (K–12, and beyond). We use the term *student* for children and adolescents in all grades. We use the term *student work* to refer to things students produce, usually in response to a teacher's assignment. The term *protocol* is applied to facilitated conversations about student work that involve multiple steps and guidelines for participation.

ACKNOWLEDGMENTS

As we developed this book, many people shared with us their ideas about and experiences with looking collaboratively at student work. For this help, we thank the teachers and administrators of Belle Sherman Elementary

School, Ithaca, New York; Charles Shaw Middle School, Gorham, Maine; Fannie Lou Hamer Freedom High School, the Bronx, New York; Manhasset High School, Long Island, New York; North Shore High School, Long Island, New York; Park East High School, New York City; and Rosemont Middle School, Norfolk, Virginia.

In particular, we acknowledge the important contributions of the following teachers and administrators: John Caterina, Jean Davis, Colleen Fleming, John Giambalvo, Diane Knott, Nick Mazzarella, Jane Montagna, John Newlin, Evelyn Ort, Vicki Pearce, Lisa Purcell, Teri Schrader, Jim Silcox, Rebecca Wilusz, and Nancy Young.

Many thanks to Eric Buchovecky, Thomas Hatch, Sara Hendren, and Steven Levy, who provided us with detailed comments on earlier manuscripts of the first edition, and to Suzy Ort for her contribution to the Park East High School story in Chapter 5. We are also grateful to the members of the *Student Work* Working Group of the ATLAS Seminar.

Finally, we would like to acknowledge with gratitude the colleagues who have profoundly influenced how we think about and practice looking at student work collaboratively: Joseph McDonald, Steve Seidel, and Gene Thompson-Grove.

The first edition of this book was a product of the ATLAS Seminar, which was funded by the Spencer Foundation, the John D. and Catherine T. MacArthur Foundation, and the Rockefeller Foundation. We are grateful for their generous support.

Looking Together
at Student Work

Overview

THE FACULTY OF A SMALL HIGH SCHOOL in New York City decided to focus on student writing across the curriculum. They began by examining samples of their students' writing that came from a routine performance assessment administered by an outside organization. From there, they decided to examine writing assignments and student work from their own classrooms using a new protocol (or conversation guide) they developed to give feedback to one another.

In Virginia, a middle school had just made exhibitions (public presentations of students' long-term research projects) a requirement for students at three grade levels. The faculty needed a way to train people from outside the school to serve as judges on exhibition panels. To accomplish this goal, they designed a training session around discussing videotaped examples of student exhibitions. The judges-in-training looked at the examples and talked together about how they would have responded if they had been judges on those exhibition panels. Looking together at the student work gave them the opportunity to think through what it meant to be a judge before they had to assume that role themselves.

When a middle school in Maine began using portfolio assessment, the faculty wanted to involve students and parents in examining the work collected in the portfolios to see whether it demonstrated progress toward the students' goals for the year. The faculty and students designed a conferencing system that brought parents, student, and teacher together twice a year to review and discuss the work in each student's portfolio.

Although their situations differ, these schools share three important features:

- Each school was in the midst of important changes in the way student work was structured, presented, or assessed.
- Each school had identified a particular goal that it needed to accomplish in order to carry out the changes.
- Each school used the strategy of looking collaboratively at student work as a way of moving toward its goal. At the heart of each

strategy was a protocol, or structured way of examining and discussing both the student work and relevant teacher work.

This book is based on work done in these schools and others like them. The stories of these three schools are told in more detail in Chapter 5.

WHO IS THIS BOOK FOR?

Looking Together at Student Work is designed for schools, teachers, and administrators of all grade levels. If one or more of the following descriptions fits you and your colleagues, you may find the ideas in this book especially helpful:

- You use projects, exhibitions, or portfolios, and you want to make them more effective learning tools for your students.
- You are trying a new teaching approach or learning activity in your classroom(s) and want to look more closely at its impact on your students' work.
- You are looking for ways to talk more often and more thoughtfully with your colleagues about teaching, learning, and assessment.
- You are striving to develop a stronger professional learning community within your school.
- You are looking for ways to reflect on, discuss with others, and revise your own practice.
- You are looking for ways to talk with the broader community outside the school about the teaching, learning, and assessment going on inside your school.

WHAT DOES THIS BOOK DO?

This book is designed to provide educators (teachers, administrators, curriculum coordinators, staff developers, and others) with resources for working together to examine and discuss student work—projects, artwork, essays, and other products of class assignments. These products provide the most important evidence of student growth and learning and of the effectiveness of teachers' own practices. The resources in this book include the following:

- Steps for starting and sustaining collaborative discussions of student work

- Descriptions of three established structures, or "protocols," for guiding discussion of student work: the Tuning Protocol, the Collaborative Assessment Conference, and the Consultancy
- Examples from three schools that have developed their own ways of looking at and talking about student work
- Basic guidelines for how to facilitate protocols for looking collaboratively at student work
- A list of resources (books, articles, videos, and organizations) that can provide further help

WHAT DOESN'T THIS BOOK DO?

This book does not provide a recipe for how your school should look at and talk about student work. Nor does it provide a predetermined list of questions that you should use when looking at student work. Only you and the people with whom you work know the needs and goals of your faculty, community, and students. The examples provided here can give you a starting point, but the questions and the specific protocols you use must be identified by those most closely involved in the work—teachers and administrators.

The book does not give detailed information about how to do exhibitions, project work, portfolios, or any of the other kinds of tasks that are typically the focus of such collaborative discussions. However, the resource list at the end of the book can direct you to further reading about these topics.

It does not tell you how to develop standards, criteria, or rubrics for student work, although we believe that protocols, including some of those described in this book, are effective tools for developing and refining standards, criteria, and assessment instruments for student work.

It does not provide a blueprint for the structural changes that may accompany a school's efforts to support discussions of student work. However, you will find some practical suggestions in various chapters of the book to help you to develop such a plan.

WHAT DO WE MEAN BY STUDENT WORK?

Samples of student work are at the very heart of the processes and protocols described in this book. But what kinds of student work are useful for educators to look at collaboratively? There are two important considerations in addressing this question. The first is thinking broadly about student work: Survey all that students do in classrooms and outside them and identify the "artifacts" that provide evidence of teaching and learning. These artifacts might be process- or product-oriented, that is, drafts or finished pieces. They might be individually created or the product of group collaboration. They might be concrete and tangible, such as essays, posters, models, or lab reports, or more ephemeral, such as a class discussion or debate. They might be long term, such as a multistep research project, or on demand, such as a quiz or test.

The forms student work can take are virtually unlimited. However, in our experience, the kinds of student work that are most conducive to productive collaborative discussions of teaching and learning are those that provide a glimpse of both what and how students are learning. Such work often asks students to inquire deeply into a particular topic or question or to express their ideas and opinions about an issue. This kind of work tends to be more complex, demanding, and open ended than the typical worksheet or multiple-choice test.

The second question is one of selection: What particular samples of student work will be the most useful for addressing the purposes that a teacher or a group has identified for collaboratively looking at student work? For example, if a group is interested in how to support students' math problem-solving skills, student work selected for the discussion might include samples from several students working the same problem with different results. If a group is interested in understanding how a child's reading comprehension develops over time, it might look at excerpts from the child's reading journal over a period of several months along with running records kept by the teacher. The protocol, or structure for the conversation, will also influence the kind of work selected. In Chapter 4, we describe three commonly used protocols and list the kinds and amounts of student work typically presented in each.

HOW DO TEACHERS USUALLY LOOK AT STUDENT WORK?

Teachers have always spent a good deal of time looking at student work. They read it to provide feedback to the students who did it. They look at student work to evaluate it, assigning it a score or a grade. They examine it for clues about how to plan future curricula and assessments that will best serve the students, or to prepare for parent conferences. Many teachers consider the process of examining, assessing, and evaluating student work one of the most important—and time-consuming—aspects of their teaching. Most of this work is done by teachers individually, alone at their desks in classrooms, at their kitchen tables, even waiting in doctors' offices or at their children's basketball practice.

WHY LOOK AT STUDENT WORK COLLABORATIVELY?

Looking collaboratively at student work is not meant to replace the important ways you look at student work by yourself. However, working with others can bring to the surface resources, ideas, and strategies that make the individual efforts more productive. It is hard to imagine doctors who never consult with other physicians (or with their patients) but rather make all decisions about their patients' prognoses and treatments on their own. Like doctors, educators benefit from consultation with colleagues. In the teaching profession, student work provides some of the critical data and cases that allow professionals to work together to make the best possible decisions for their students.

In addition, there are some purposes for looking at student work that, it could be said, require collaboration and conversation—developing common standards within grade levels or departments, for example. To accomplish this aim, a school or a group of teachers must develop not only the standards but also a shared understanding of what those standards mean and how to apply them to students' work. In our experience, examining and discussing samples of student work is virtually the only way to achieve such a goal.

HOW MANY PEOPLE DOES IT TAKE TO "LOOK TOGETHER"?

Sometimes, "looking together" means that a whole school is engaged in a particular process or strategy for examining student work. More often, such collaboration begins with a small group—typically from three to eight teachers or administrators or both—who have a common interest: They want to find out more about the kinds of problems that 4th graders are having in math. Or they want to consider how to improve the 11th-grade writing course. Or they want to get ideas from one another about how to organize and assess portfolios in their classrooms. One person in the group serves as facilitator, a role we discuss in Chapter 6. Of course, it also takes people who are not necessarily "at the table" to make this kind of work possible: Administrators and teacher leaders must champion the work and provide the time and support required so that it can be done regularly and well.

HOW MUCH TIME DOES IT TAKE TO HOLD COLLABORATIVE DISCUSSIONS OF STUDENT WORK?

Collaborative discussions take more time than it takes to look at a single piece of student work by yourself. How much more depends on your group's particular goals for looking at the work and on the protocols you use. Some goals (establishing common standards about student work, for example) may take only one or two sessions a year. Other goals (such as finding out more about the learning styles and needs of individual students) require more frequent meetings—anywhere from once a week to once a month to four or five times a year. The duration of these meetings also varies according to their purpose. Typical meetings last from 45 minutes to an hour and a half. Some schools have benefited from half- or full-day meetings focused on examining student work.

Finding this kind of time is not easy. Schools are not typically structured to support professional collaboration: Rigid bell schedules, limited planning time, and the sheer number of students in a single teacher's load all work against thoughtful and productive collaboration. Nor has teaching developed some of the forms of evidence-based collaboration typical of other professions—consultations with colleagues, case reviews, and conferences. Indeed, it is unusual for anybody besides the teacher, the student, and occasionally a parent to examine any given piece of that student's work, let alone to comment on it or raise questions about it or learn from it.

WHY USE A "PROTOCOL"?

Why not just start talking? Protocols, such as the Collaborative Assessment Conference, the Consultancy, and the Tuning Protocol, provide structures for conversations about student work. They ask participants, including the presenter, to go through a number of steps in a fixed order. For example, in the Tuning Protocol, the presenter's description of context is followed by "clarifying questions" from other participants. Such structures prompt participants to offer certain kinds of comments (such as descriptions, questions, or judgments).

While some people find protocols artificial, at least at first, our experience and research suggest that the structure for the conversation provides a safe, supportive environment for educators to share publicly their students' work and their own—something they don't typically do. Protocols also encourage participants to offer substantive feedback to their colleague(s)—again, something that doesn't happen often in the professional lives of teachers and administrators. They provide teachers with a set time and a forum for individual and group reflection on student work, student learning, and their own teaching. They help avoid quick judgments about student work. With so many pressing concerns competing for teachers' and administrators' time, the protocols help a group stay focused on the essentials of teaching and learning for at least 45 minutes at a time. In the hurly-burly of teaching, this is both a luxury and a necessity.

WHAT DOES THE RESEARCH SAY ABOUT LOOKING TOGETHER AT STUDENT WORK?

Using protocols to look at student work has grown in popularity and become more common among educators in the years since the first edition of this book was published. During that time, a number of excellent resources that support collaborative examination of and reflection on student work have been developed (many of these are included in the List of Resources at the end of the book). In the same period, a research base has emerged that supports the value of looking together at student work in improving teaching and learning.

A few years ago, Judith Warren Little and her colleagues (2003)* published a review of research on school-based initiatives that incorporate various approaches to the collaborative examination of student work. They found that "looking at student work has the potential to expand teachers' opportunity to learn, to cultivate a professional community that is both willing and able to inquire into practice, and to focus school-based teacher conversations on the improvement of teaching and learning" (p. 192).

As yet, no large-scale studies show that using protocols for looking at student work increases student achievement on standardized tests—a dubious proxy for actual learning. However, a recent study of schools in Chicago conducted by Penny Sebring, Anthony Bryk, and colleagues (Sebring, Allensworth, Bryk, Easton, & Luppescu, 2006) demonstrates that a strong school-based professional community (with features like those described by Little and colleagues) along with other critical ingredients (including leadership, ambitious instruction, and school-community ties) leads to improved student outcomes, including "enhanced student engagement and expanded academic learning" (p. 13). A study by Fred Newmann and Associates (1996) showed that "strong professional communities in [study schools] enhanced teachers' attention to the intellectual quality of student learning and their commitment to the restructuring effort" (p. 184).

In a study of Boston public high schools' reform efforts, Barbara Neufeld and Katrina Woodworth (2000) found that those schools with "high functioning" instructional leadership teams and looking-at-student-work groups

---

*All works cited in this book appear in the List of Resources.

had "better established collegial, collaborative, instructionally-focused cultures" than schools with less well functioning leadership teams and groups that did not engage in regular looking-at-student-work practices (p. 9). The authors state that teachers in these higher-functioning groups demonstrated a willingness to "make themselves vulnerable by sharing student work that was far below their expectations" (p. 47).

While more studies are needed that investigate outcomes—for teachers and students—of ongoing collaborative examination of student work, research consistently demonstrates the value that teachers themselves attach to opportunities to collaborate with colleagues in examining and reflecting on teaching and learning within their classrooms. However, for most teachers and administrators in most schools, such opportunities are still too rare and too piecemeal.

SUMMARY

Much will have to change about schooling as we know it to support a truly collaborative working environment for teachers. But even without fundamental changes, some teachers and administrators have begun to find ways to work together to look at and learn from samples of student work. In writing and revising this book we have drawn on the experiences of many of these teachers and administrators, as well as those of the facilitators, university educators, and researchers who have worked with them. Our goal in the book is to support all educators as they develop their own approaches to professional collaboration that focus on the work that students and teachers do every day in their classrooms.

CHAPTER 2

Developing a Way of Looking Together at Student Work

TEACHING WELL IS REALLY a cyclical process. It requires setting goals, planning, and continuous evaluation and adjustment, as well as the interaction with students that is its heart. Examining student work is an important and complex part of teaching, yet there are few resources to support it. The steps that follow are offered as one such resource. They describe how some groups of teachers and administrators have begun to use protocols in an ongoing way to examine their students' work collaboratively. These steps include the following:

1. Taking stock of current ways of looking at student work
2. Establishing goals and framing questions
3. Choosing, adapting, or developing a protocol for looking collaboratively at student work
4. Using the protocol over the course of several meetings
5. Periodically reflecting on the goals and framing questions and revising how the group is using the protocol to address those goals and questions.

Like teaching itself, the process of looking collaboratively at student work over time is not linear, but cyclical. When group members have worked through several protocols, they return to their initial goals and questions, revising them as needed and fine-tuning their use of protocols to better focus on those aims. Having developed a deeper understanding of what they are looking for and how to look, the group then resumes the process of examining student work through protocols. A representation of this process is shown in Figure 2.1.

Although experiences differ for every group that undertakes a collaborative examination of student work, some commonalties emerge. For each

Figure 2.1. A Process for Looking Collaboratively at Student Work

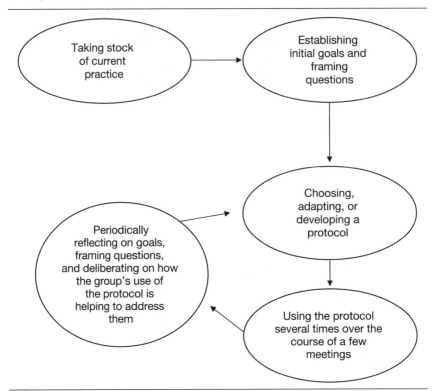

of the steps, we have offered some lessons from teachers' experiences in brief sections titled "Moving to Practice." We have also included some brief examples from schools engaged in looking at student work.

TAKING STOCK OF CURRENT WAYS OF LOOKING AT STUDENT WORK

Schools never start from scratch in collaboratively examining student work. Teachers have always looked individually at their students' work to assess student achievement and progress. In planning to work collaboratively, look for examples of how teachers currently examine student work and consider how these practices might be adapted or expanded. For example, if students regularly make public presentations of their project work to parents and classmates, a group of teachers might arrange to attend these presentations and then to discuss them afterward. Taking stock of current practices can bring to the surface some of the questions and issues that are not addressed in how student work is currently treated.

> In one elementary school, each student traditionally met regularly with her teacher to work on a set of math problems. These conferences formed part of each child's math portfolio that was used for assessment purposes. At these meetings, the student had the list of problems in front of her; the teacher sat next to her or across the table and noted how she worked the problems, sometimes asking the student questions about how she had done her work. "We're not just interested in whether they got the answer right, but how. Do they use their fingers? Work on scratch paper? Ask for help?" One teacher decided to videotape the conferences. When the faculty as a whole began meeting to look at students' math work, the videotapes provided a particularly effective focus for teachers' discussions about teaching math problem-solving and individualizing instruction.

Moving to Practice

Consider the ways in which you (and others within your school) currently examine student work either individually or collaboratively. For example, do you review portfolios together, sit in on one another's student exhibitions, or score work with a common rubric?

There may be resistance to—or skepticism about—trying a new way of looking at student work with colleagues, especially if people in the school are used to their own ways of doing so. Is the new process meeting a genuine need? Does it allow everyone to enter into a new approach in a way that is comfortable for him or her?

ESTABLISHING GOALS AND FRAMING QUESTIONS

The purposes for examining and discussing student work are many and varied. Some common ones include the following:

- Learning more about an individual child's response to an assignment
- Setting standards for all students' performances
- Learning about your own teaching and assessment practices

- Honing observational and interpretive skills, which can be used in the classroom as well as within protocols
- Developing a common language or criteria for discussing teaching and learning

Being clear about the purpose for looking at student work will help your group to select the most appropriate protocol or guide the group in developing its own. (It is not always easy—indeed, not always possible—to articulate goals at the beginning of a process. At the end of this chapter, we offer an alternative to starting off with well-articulated goals.)

Broad goals, like those mentioned above, are usually established through conversations prior to engaging in the examination of student work. In these preliminary conversations, participants address questions such as:

- What aspects of our curriculum or instruction do we need to focus on?
- What kinds of information do we need to make good decisions about curriculum and instruction (beyond the information that test scores and grades typically provide)?

These conversations might take place within a teaching team, at a department meeting, or within a study group or "critical friends group." Often, one person on the faculty acts as the catalyst or champion, calling a group's attention to the learning opportunity afforded by looking together at student work. In other cases, collaboratively examining student work may be an explicit part of a school's strategy for professional development, use of data, or school improvement.

The faculty of a new small high school with a bilingual student body struggled with how to make language development a focus for the whole school: how to get all teachers involved in teaching reading, writing, and speaking. One teacher asked, "What if we have students keep language portfolios in their humanities class, but when it comes to evaluating them, involve the entire faculty and administration in reading and responding to them? Then when we come together in team meetings we can look at the portfolios and the response letters we write to students, and really talk about our students' language development and what we're doing to support it." Here, the school's goal was clear: making language development more central to the work of the entire faculty. Looking at student work (by collectively examining and discussing students' language portfolios) became one tool for accomplishing that goal.

To achieve the initial agreement, participants must be open to other perspectives, listen to each other, and discuss individual interests and concerns. But reaching initial agreement is just the beginning: Determining the broad goals for looking collaboratively at student work should be a cyclical process, in which participants agree on their questions; get involved in addressing those questions by looking at student work; and emerge with greater clarity about the questions, leading them to revise the initial question or to articulate others.

Once you have an idea of the broad area of concern, it is important to narrow the focus. Many groups have found it helpful to frame one or two "focusing questions"—questions that help the group concentrate on a particular aspect of the student work or assignment being presented. The most important questions usually come from those who actually present their work or that of their students for collaborative examination; typically, these specific questions are strongly related to schoolwide questions and broad concerns of the faculty.

> Carolyn, a high school English teacher, had assigned a large-scale independent research project for the first time. She struggled with the widely varied quality of the papers that her students produced. Her department had recently set aside time once a month to look at student work collaboratively as one way to support the department members in the ongoing development of their teaching skills. When Carolyn brought in her students' papers for the group to look at, she also brought a focusing question: "How can I provide supportive, individualized instruction without taking away from students' ownership of their topics and their learning about independent research?"—a focusing question that dovetailed with the group members' broader goal of helping one another to improve teaching.

There are probably as many types of questions as there are educators. In Figure 2.2 we present some categories of questions that you may want to consider as you move from the group's broad questions to framing your own more specific ones for examining student work.

Moving to Practice

It may take some time for the group to reach agreement about the goals it wants to achieve through examining student work. As the group begins to articulate its key goals and focusing questions, consider the following issues: Is looking at student work collaboratively an appropriate strategy for addressing the group's goals and questions? Are there too many purposes on the table

Figure 2.2. Questions That Might Guide the Examination of Student Work

---

About the quality of student work:

- Is the work good enough, that is, does it meet our expectations for high-quality work?
- What is "good enough," and how can we illustrate good work for students?
- In what ways does this work meet or fail to meet a particular set of criteria or standards?
- What are the most effective forms of assessment for figuring out whether work is meeting standards and for giving students useful feedback?

About teaching practice:

- What do the students' responses indicate about the effectiveness of a prompt or assignment? How might the assignment be improved to support high-quality student performance?
- What kinds of instruction support high-quality student performance?

About students' understanding:

- What does this work tell us about how well the student understands the topic of the assignment?
- What initial understandings do we see beginning to emerge in this work?

About students' growth:

- How does this range of work from a single student demonstrate growth (in _____) over time?
- How can I support student growth (in _____) more effectively?

About students' intent:

- What issues or questions is this student focused on?
- What aspects of the assignment intrigued this student?
- Into which parts of the assignment did the student put the most effort?
- To what extent is the student challenging him- or herself? In what ways?

---

for the group to focus on? (One or two main goals or questions are usually plenty.) Do members of the group seem to have fundamentally different ideas about the purposes for looking at student work? Do the questions you want to ask seem too narrow (too small) or unanswerable (too large)?

An Alternative Approach

Getting clear about purpose is not always straightforward or easy. Within every school there exist different—sometimes competing—perspectives on teaching and learning goals and methods. If the group is unsure of its goals or is in danger of spending too much time trying to come to initial agreement, you might want to use the "let's try it and see what happens" approach. Rather than articulating specific goals initially, your group can decide to make the initial goal very general—perhaps even vague.

For example, several teachers might decide that they would like a little more time for reflecting on what is happening in their classrooms. Or they might decide that they would like to have more structure for their conversations during faculty meetings or in team planning time. Looking collaboratively at student work would be a way to accomplish either of these very general goals.

Inevitably, looking together at student work raises a host of thoughts, questions, and concerns. From these issues that emerge over successive uses of the protocols, the group members may be able to articulate more crisply and specifically the goals they would like to pursue. They could then decide to refine the protocol they are using, to achieve those goals more effectively, or they might decide that such goals require an entirely different protocol and adopt or develop one of their own.

CHOOSING, ADAPTING, OR DEVELOPING A PROTOCOL FOR LOOKING COLLABORATIVELY AT STUDENT WORK

Once you have established (more or less) the purposes for examining student work together or have articulated questions to explore, you can identify a protocol that will help you achieve your ends. A number of such protocols are currently in use. Three of them are described in detail in Chapter 4:

- *The Tuning Protocol.* Developed by Joseph McDonald and colleagues in the early 1990s for the Coalition of Essential Schools, the Tuning Protocol is a structured, facilitated conversation that asks participants to provide the presenter(s) with feedback—both "warm" and "cool"—on a project; task; or assessment tool, such as a rubric. At the heart of the process is an examination of student work samples.
- *The Collaborative Assessment Conference.* The Collaborative Assessment Conference was developed in 1988 by Steve Seidel and colleagues at Harvard Project Zero. The Collaborative Assessment Conference invites participants to look at, describe, and ask questions about pieces of student work to develop a deeper understanding of the student who created it, of that student's interests and strengths, and of the teaching/learning environment.

- *The Consultancy.* This protocol was developed by Gene Thompson-Grove and colleagues at the National School Reform Faculty in the 1990s. It is designed to help groups examine a professional dilemma. The goal is not to solve the dilemma (since dilemmas, by their nature, are usually not solvable), but to help the presenter and the group members to expand their thinking about the nature and ramifications of the dilemma. Possible suggestions for managing the dilemma often emerge, but the conversation is just as likely to lead to a new formulation of the problem.

Other processes currently used include the following:

- The Descriptive Review of the Child, and other descriptive review processes, developed by Patricia Carini and colleagues at the Prospect Center in Vermont
- The Primary Language Record, developed by the Centre for Language in Primary Education in London
- The Standards in Practice protocol, developed by the Education Trust in Washington, D.C.

For more about these and other protocols for looking collaboratively at student work, see the List of Resources.

Although protocols differ in practical ways (the time they typically take to complete, the number of samples of student work they typically have as their focus, and so on), there are two crucial aspects to which you should pay particular attention as you choose or develop a protocol:

- *Mode of looking.* The degree to which the protocol encourages participants to describe, interpret, or evaluate the work being presented. Some protocols emphasize description; others have a focus on evaluation.
- *Context.* The way and extent to which the protocol makes room for presentation of the work's context (background information about the student who created the work, the assignment and conditions under which it was carried out, and so on). Some protocols begin with the presenter describing the context; others call for the presenter to share the context only after the group has examined the work; in yet others, the context is never presented.

More than any other factors, these two, mode of looking and context, will influence the flavor of the group's conversation, the kinds of issues that emerge during the conversation, and the kinds of goals the conversation will enable the group to reach. In Chapter 3, we consider these two aspects of protocol design in more detail.

Moving to Practice

Group members will need to consider which protocol they want to use. Starting with an already-established protocol, rather than immediately developing your own, can be helpful; however, deciding exactly which protocol is the right one to start with may not be easy.

After using a particular protocol a few times, group members may discuss other protocols they want to try. Is there agreement about trying a new protocol? Has the original protocol been given a fair try? The group may need to carry out a protocol several times before participants can tell how well it is helping them move toward their goals.

USING A PROTOCOL OVER TIME

No matter which protocol you use, you will need to address important practical issues in order to carry out that protocol. We have divided these issues into two categories: key questions and logistics.

Key Questions

Who Will Be Involved in Looking Collaboratively at Student Work? Participants might include teachers, administrators, parents, students, colleagues from other schools, and representatives from the community (such as teachers from local colleges, community leaders, and business people). Other options include deciding whether to organize groups within or across grade levels, subject areas, schools in the district, or a combination of these. Teachers and administrators naturally may want to keep the discussion "within the family." For many purposes this makes good sense, but consider what might be learned from informed and sympathetic outsiders. In the words of one high school principal,

> We always learn more when we involve different people in looking at student work. It may take more effort to organize those meetings, but the result is always of higher quality.

Who Will Present Student Work? Everyone can learn from presenting, but no one should be forced to present. Some teachers will be more comfortable than others in presenting their students' work. Pairs or teams of teachers may present together, and often this approach reduces stress for the presenting team. If the idea of presenting your student work seems daunting, it may help to remember that the structure of the protocol and the facilitation create a safe atmosphere in which to talk about issues related to practice. As one high school special education teacher put it,

> I was nervous about presenting my students' work, but as soon as people started talking, I could relax, because they saw the good things about my kids and they helped me see some things I could do differently.

In any case, the presentation should be seen as conversational rather than rehearsed. Ideally, over time, everyone in the group will have the opportunity to present work.

What Kind of Student Work Will Be Presented? The kind of student work presented will best be determined by the purposes and questions you define. Particular protocols, too, may lend themselves to different kinds of work. For example, the Collaborative Assessment Conference is often used with a single piece of work, and the Tuning Protocol for examination of multiple samples. Whatever protocol you use, here are some issues for the presenter (in consultation with the facilitator) to consider in choosing student work:

- *Work that piques your curiosity.* Choosing a piece or collection of student work about which you have a genuine question will help to ensure a productive conversation. Is there a piece or body of student work that raises a question for you? Are you wondering how to improve an assignment that was not particularly successful? Would you like the perspectives of others on the work of a student you feel you do not understand or appreciate as well as you would like? Check with the facilitator about when and how you should share your questions with the group.
- *Number of pieces of work.* Do you want to look at a single piece of work? Several drafts of a single piece? Several pieces from different students? Several pieces from the same student (perhaps completed at different times in the year)? Again, it will be helpful to consult with the facilitator in making this decision, since he or she will have a feel for the kind and amount of work best served by the protocol you will be using. (See Chapter 4 for more detail.)

- *Quality or level of the work.* Do you want to share a polished piece, a rough draft, or perhaps several drafts and the finished piece? Do you want to bring the very best piece of the batch or a piece that fell short of your expectations?
- *Context for the work.* How much context is called for by the protocol in which you will be participating? If the protocol is one in which the work's context is shared, you might want to make some notes for yourself about what you want to say. (Review the protocol schedule or check with the group facilitator to find out how much time you'll have to say it.) You might want to describe the objectives for the assignment, the amount of time the students had to carry it out, how the project or task was organized, the evaluation criteria, and so on. Bring copies of any context-related documents (the assignment sheet, the scoring rubric, description of objectives) that you might want to share with the group.
- *Sharing the work in the meeting.* How will everyone in the group be able to examine the work? Discuss this in advance with the facilitator so that the two of you can work out the logistics ahead of time. In Figure 2.3 we offer some suggestions for making different kinds of work easily accessible for group examination.

What About Students' Rights to Confidentiality? Respecting students' ownership of their work and their right to control who sees it and how it is used is essential. Typically, students produce schoolwork assuming that only their teacher (and perhaps a few classmates or family members) will see it. For sharing student work within the school, the faculty and administration should establish a policy that addresses confidentiality issues. Such a policy might include, for example, asking the students' permission to share their work. Students often appreciate the fact that you take their work seriously enough to want to discuss it with other teachers. They also may want to hear something about what other people had to say about it.

If you plan to take the work outside the school building, it is a good idea to ask the student or the parent or guardian (depending on the age of the student) to sign a release form that gives permission for the work to be shared publicly. If you have no way of obtaining permission from the student or the parents, remove the student's name from the work and take every precaution not to reveal his or her identity in the course of the conversation. (You may want to take this step even if you have the student's and parent's or guardian's permission, to err on the side of confidentiality.) Finally, remember that using videos or photographs of children raises important confidentiality concerns.

Figure 2.3. Making Student Work Accessible for Group Examination:
Tips for the Presenter

Written work:

Try to have copies for everyone, especially if the piece is longer than a page. If
you do not have copies and the writing is brief, you might try reading it out
loud two or three times for the group. For especially long pieces, you might
want to focus only on particular sections. You might also invite different group
members to examine different sections of a longer work and then to describe it
for the whole group.

Two-dimensional artwork:

If the artwork is small, try to make copies. If the artwork is in color and the
copies are black and white, bring the original with you so that people can refer
to it for more detail.

Three-dimensional work:

For posterboard displays, dioramas, models, and similar kinds of three-
dimensional work, set up the piece in a central location where all the
participants can see it. If the group is large, it might be useful to set it up just
before the meeting, so that participants can have a chance to examine it closely
while they are waiting for the meeting to begin.

Video:

If you want to show a video of student work, choose the clip carefully; a 5- to
7-minute piece is usually as much as a group can work with in a typical
meeting of an hour to an hour and a half. The group may need to see the clip(s)
twice in order to discuss the student work in detail. (A transcript can be
helpful.) Be sure to let the facilitator know ahead of time that you want to use
video so that he or she can arrange to have video equipment at the meeting.
The presenter may also need to orient the group briefly about which point in
the lesson or activity the clip comes from.

Logistics

When Will You Meet? If the examination of student work is to become a regular practice, how can it be given a regular slot in the school's
schedule? Can groups meet to look at student work on release days? During team planning time? During department meetings or study group
meetings? Assess how meeting time is currently used. What could be

handled in another way (for example, printing a set of announcements for everyone rather than spending 20 minutes of a meeting reading them out loud) so that examining student work can take place?

It is important to find not only enough time but also the right time:

> So much depends on the particular day when people can meet. We did a Tuning Protocol before a long weekend that was much better than in the middle of the week. . . . Or we meet in the evening when people can have dinner. (high school teacher)

Where Will You Meet? Faculty room, classroom, auditorium? Since most meetings involve 10 or fewer participants, it makes sense to look for a comfortable space with enough room in which to spread out materials—and equipment, such as video players—but not so much that the group feels dwarfed:

> We used to use a classroom after school, but then for some reason we had to find a new place. We moved to the band room. Something about being in a different space, a more special one, made a big difference. (middle school teacher and group leader)

Who Will Facilitate? All the protocols described in this book require a facilitator, someone to keep the group focused on the task and make sure the structure and guidelines of the process are followed. As a middle school teacher pointed out,

> I learned a lot about teaching from facilitating meetings. I think it's important for the facilitator to stay in that role, even if he's dying to jump in with comments or questions for the presenting teacher. The group needs somebody who can make sure everybody is heard.

Everyone can learn to facilitate, but not everyone will feel comfortable doing so, especially the first few times the group meets. It takes practice as well as cooperation from the full group. Some groups have found it helpful to have a facilitator from outside the group, at least for the first few times. Some groups rotate facilitation among themselves. (See Chapter 6 for more suggestions about facilitation.)

Moving to Practice

As you begin to talk about the student work, unforeseen issues and questions will arise. You may start out looking at how a student's work rates on the criteria or rubric and shift to discussing whether the rubric is adequate for the kinds of work students are producing. Such issues are important, and discovering them is one of the great benefits of looking collaboratively at student work. However, it is easy to start out talking about a student's work and end up talking about something incidental, for example, a field trip the student's class took recently. The facilitator and the group must decide whether these emergent issues or questions should be discussed immediately or noted for later attention.

The protocol that guides the conversation should help the group to keep to its stated goals and focusing questions. However, if you are facilitating, be aware that some people may react negatively or ambivalently to the artificial structure that such a protocol imposes on the discussion. It is useful to recognize this but important not to give up on the structure the group has decided upon. Instead, go through the protocol as planned and save time afterward for a debriefing discussion (see "Reflecting on and Revising the Goals and the Protocols," below). Often, discussion with colleagues helps those who are most critical of the structure to see its value. In Chapter 6 we offer further thoughts on the challenges of facilitation.

REFLECTING ON AND REVISING THE GOALS
AND THE PROTOCOLS

After several rounds of looking at student work collaboratively, groups need time to reflect on and discuss several questions:

- What are we learning through this process about our initial goals and questions? Do the goals need to be refined? Have new questions emerged?
- How can the group's use of protocols be improved so that it helps to achieve the goal(s) more effectively?
- How does our use of protocols connect or relate to other staff development or program development initiatives in the school? Can connections be explored or fostered that will strengthen teaching and learning across the school?

Learning Through Protocols

When educators meet to look at and discuss student work, everybody learns. Sometimes the lessons are very direct: "Now I know how to work with students on this particular problem." Often, though, the learning is more general: "I see the need to be much clearer with students about the criteria." Much of this learning becomes personal as group members, the presenter as well as others, reflect on what they have learned about their own students, standards, and practice over the course of several protocols.

> A high school teachers' group on Friday afternoon had just completed a process focused on examining student research papers. The teachers' reflections on the session revealed the variety in what they had learned from it. The presenting teacher commented, "There is so much out there on the table now for me to think about, like what you [another teacher in the group] said about audience." Another teacher made the connection to her own practice: "I'm thinking about my science investigations with students and this whole issue of how much to intervene."

Often, such learning leads to new questions or to revisions of the original goals and questions. Time is needed in which the group can deliberate and develop revised goals and questions that more accurately reflect the issues they feel are most central to their work as educators.

Improving the Group's Use of Protocols

It is also important for participants to consider what they have learned about the protocol(s) for examining student work: What worked? What should change? Is this the right protocol for achieving the group's goals? In some cases, answering these questions will lead to changing the protocol or developing a new one.

As your group gets more familiar with a particular protocol through repeated use, you might consider loosening the structure a bit. Adhering to the structure of a particular protocol in early meetings can give way to more open discussion as trust develops within the group. In the beginning, the structure of a particular protocol helps the group to focus its discussion on the student work rather than on the host of issues—schedules, availability of books or curriculum materials, the limited planning time available to teachers, and so on—that will inevitably arise in the course of the discussion. Through practice, groups incorporate into their discussions the principles behind the structured protocol, perhaps making the rigor of that structure less essential:

> We needed the practice of going through the structured process. We couldn't have leaped to having this level of discussion [without it]. (high school department coordinator)

Supporting Reflection

Reflection is an important part of every protocol and can occur through discussion or writing, usually at the end of each meeting. Most protocols, including the Collaborative Assessment Conference, the Tuning Protocol, and the Consultancy—have built-in opportunities for reflection both on what was learned and on the process itself.

> A high school teacher, after participating in a Tuning Protocol with teachers from many schools, reflected, "I didn't feel like we really had time to look at the student work. We need more time to really look through it, read one student's paper twice, maybe, before we can really say anything about it." This feedback was useful to teachers in planning future sessions.

Even with this regular opportunity to reflect at the end of each protocol, it is important periodically to set aside more extended time—perhaps a whole meeting—for stepping back and reflecting on the group's work as a whole. You might want to draw on some of the following reflection questions to get you started:

- What have we been learning that relates to our original goal or question?
- What other questions, goals, and issues seem to be emerging over the course of our work together?
- What has worked well in our protocol-based conversations?
- How have our discussions related to other school issues?
- Have we actually focused on students' work or on other issues?
- Have we been following the protocol as we planned to? If not, why?
- How could our use of the protocol be improved to better achieve our goals?
- How can we build on our past conversations to make examining student work a more frequent and important part of our own work?

CONNECTING THE USE OF PROTOCOLS
TO OTHER INITIATIVES

Using protocols for looking at student work collaboratively is never the only form of staff development or program development going on within a school—nor should it be. Sometimes using protocols will be initiated as a way to further a school's staff development goals, for example, in integrating writing across the curriculum. At other times, the connection between seemingly separate initiatives may be discovered after the work is under way. Taking time to reflect on the use of protocols can uncover ways that complementary efforts can reinforce each other. For example, a group's examination of student problem-solving strategies might lead to a staff development session on how to support and assess problem solving in the classroom.

Moving to Practice

Groups should give themselves time to reflect together on their work: Are they learning about their students as well as about their own practice as educators? Do group members leave meetings with information, ideas, and agreement about what to do next?

Discussing student work sometimes brings out conflicting beliefs and assumptions about the kinds of work students should do, about how students' work should be assessed, about individual students' abilities and motivations, and about the ways teachers should teach. Is the facilitator aware of conflict as it arises? How do the facilitator and the group strive to maintain an honest, productive, and nonjudgmental discussion? (See Chapter 6 for more on facilitation skills.)

CHAPTER 3

Crucial Considerations: Description, Interpretation, Evaluation, and Context

NO TWO PROTOCOLS FOR looking at student work are quite the same. Some are effective for large groups, some for smaller groups. Some are designed to support looking at many samples of student work at once, some invite focusing on only one or two pieces, and so on. However, there are two aspects of protocol design that deserve special attention:

- *The mode of looking.* The degree to which the protocol encourages participants to "describe" or "interpret" or "evaluate" the work being presented
- *The role of context.* Whether and how the protocol allows for the presentation of the context of the work (that is, background information about the student who created the work, the assignment, the classroom conditions under which it was carried out, and so on)

In this chapter we will discuss each of these aspects and how it can shape the conversation depending on how it is used.

DESCRIPTION, INTERPRETATION, OR EVALUATION?

How do description, interpretation, and evaluation differ? Consider these brief definitions and examples:

Description involves identifying in very literal terms various aspects of the work being observed. Generally, there is little disagreement among group members about comments that are truly descriptive. Descriptive comments from a group that is examining a piece of student art might sound like this:

- I see a yellow circle.
- I see that the yellow circle is surrounded by blue.
- The page is fully colored—there is no white space left.

Interpretation involves assigning some meaning or intent to what is in the work. For example, the following comments involve interpretation (or speculation):

- There's a sun in a deep blue sky.
- I see a full moon in the night sky.
- That yellow circle looks like a round, shiny UFO in outer space.
- I think that the student was afraid of leaving any blank space on the page.
- I can tell that this was done by a boy from the way the spaceship is drawn.

Evaluation attaches value or personal preference to the work being examined. For example:

- The sun is drawn skillfully.
- I see a very creative student at work here.
- I really like the way she filled up the whole page.*

How Are These Different "Modes of Looking" Used?

All such comments have their place and value. However, many of the protocols for looking at student work give particular emphasis to one or more of these kinds of comments and so require participants in that protocol to distinguish carefully among them. Some protocols, such as the Collaborative Assessment Conference, give clear directions for participants to describe

---

*Thanks to Steve Seidel for permission to elaborate on the examples he presented in "Learning from Looking," in N. Lyons, ed., *With Portfolio in Hand* (New York: Teachers College Press, 1998), pp. 69–89.

what they see in the work before they interpret or speculate about the meaning of what they see. The Collaborative Assessment Conference never invites evaluation. As a result, conversations guided by the Collaborative Assessment Protocol are often more open ended, raising issues and questions for the group to consider together.

Other protocols explicitly ask participants to make evaluative comments. For example, the Tuning Protocol invites "warm" feedback, meaning feedback that identifies strengths in the work, and "cool" feedback, which identifies gaps or areas of weakness. Both warm and cool feedback are types of evaluation. Depending on the focusing question, these judgments may be about the design of the assignment or project, or about the student work itself. (In fact, any process that involves measuring students' efforts against particular criteria will require the participants to articulate some evaluations.) The prominence of evaluation makes discussions guided by the Tuning Protocol—or similar protocols—more focused on solving specific problems than on exploring a broad array of issues or questions.

The Consultancy is neither primarily descriptive nor evaluative, but rather asks participants to interpret the dilemma they have heard the presenter describe. In some cases, suggestions offered by participants might be seen as (or might actually be) evaluative.

What's Challenging About Making Distinctions?

Distinguishing among description, interpretation, and evaluation is not always easy, even when a particular protocol spells out very specifically which kind of response participants should offer. An apparently straightforward description—such as identifying colors in a piece of artwork—can start to seem like interpretation when one person's orange looks brown or red to other observers of the work. In examining a piece of student writing, one person may feel that a comment about the "bad spelling" is an objective description; another may feel that such a comment is clearly evaluative. Rather than thinking of these three kinds of responses as hard-and-fast categories, it might be helpful to imagine description, interpretation, and evaluation arrayed along a continuum. Comments can be more or less descriptive, more or less interpretive, more or less evaluative. Over time, groups usually develop their own collective sense of what kinds of comments are appropriate for specific protocols.

Of these three types of responses, interpretations and evaluations come easily for most. By contrast, description—specific, literal, careful description—often proves more challenging. In "Learning from Looking," Steve Seidel (1988a) offers thoughts about why:

I suspect that two tendencies in our culture mix dangerously and make what should be a simple act of description far more difficult than one might anticipate. First, we tend to move very quickly and rarely stop to dwell at length on what is before our eyes. A trip to a museum to watch people looking at the art often confirms that most of us spend very little time looking at a single painting. Face to face with a Rembrandt, an extraordinary opportunity to observe the work of a master, to dwell on what many consider a major accomplishment of Western culture . . . most of us spend little more than a minute or two.

Further, we seem to be in the habit of making very quick judgments, even of things that might benefit from some reflection. We often expect of ourselves and our companions that we will know our thoughts, feelings, and opinions of a film before we've even crossed the street outside the theater. Exemplified by the film critics' Siskel and Ebert's "thumbs up" or "thumbs down," there is a "let's look at it once, declare it good or bad, and get on to the next" mentality that dominates our behavior perhaps a bit more than we might like to admit. (p. 84)

To these general cultural tendencies are added the pressures and norms of the teaching profession. It is, in fact, part of an educator's responsibility to identify what students are doing well and what they're doing poorly, and to address the wrongs quickly so that individual students don't fall behind in the curriculum that has to be covered. Circumstances often force everyone who works in education into the habit of making fast, almost automatic, evaluations when looking at student work.

But many protocols for looking together at student work are designed to help everyone slow down. These protocols invite participants to take a step back and to look calmly, carefully, and patiently in order to see what the student put into the work—before attaching personal interpretations and evaluations to it. Protocols that focus on description are not always the most appropriate way to accomplish the group's goals. However, given its often surprising benefits, your group might want to consider experimenting with such a protocol rather than relying wholly on ones that emphasize interpretation and evaluation. In fact, participating in more descriptive protocols can help participants give more substantive and specific feedback when they do use protocols that focus on evaluation.

Because being descriptive without bringing in interpretation or evaluation is, initially, so challenging, some groups find it helpful to practice a brief activity that focuses on the distinction before beginning a protocol. For example, the facilitator might pick out an object in the room, say, a poster, and ask participants to carefully observe the object and then to write down five or so descriptive comments without evaluating and interpreting. In pairs or as a group, the participants parse their comments: Which ones are purely descriptive? Which involve some degree of evaluation or interpretation?

Why Do These Distinctions Matter?

In their first encounters with protocols that involve description, many teachers and administrators become frustrated with the apparent "triviality" of the conversation. In other protocols that require participants to distinguish between interpretation and evaluation, similar frustrations can emerge: What does it matter, really, if one is evaluating the work rather than offering interpretations of its meaning?

There are at least two reasons for honoring these distinctions when they appear in protocols and for incorporating them into protocols you might develop. First, as we have illustrated, the mode of looking will influence the kind of conversation a group has and will determine the goals the group can achieve together.

Second, by requiring distinctions in the kinds of responses participants make to student work, protocols enable them to develop a greater consciousness of what, exactly, in the student work they are responding to. In most protocols, the point of making these distinctions is usually not to get participants to develop perfectly descriptive or perfectly evaluative responses. Rather, attending to these distinctions helps participants to develop an awareness of their own "automatic" or "natural" responses to student work, which may involve assumptions that have no or little relation to the actual work the students have done.

With practice, many rewards come from attending in such detail to particular aspects of student work and how individuals and groups respond to it. Among those rewards are a renewed sensitivity to the complexity of students' thinking and more finely honed observational skills when looking at student work with and without colleagues.

CONTEXT

By *context* we mean all the background information about the work being presented, the assignment that gave rise to it, and the student(s) who created it. What was the assignment? How was it graded? What criteria or rubrics were used to assess it? How much time were students given to work on it? What resources were available? Is this the kind of work the student usually does? Did the student seem to have difficulty with any part of it or seem to put a lot of effort into it? Did the student do this work at school or at home? Alone or in collaboration with a partner or group? Was help available at home? What did the student have to say about it while working on it and after it was completed? All these concerns are part of the work's context.

How Is Presentation of Context Used in Protocols?

Whether and how context is presented to a group gathered to examine the work is a matter that varies according to the protocol being used. Some protocols call for the presenter to describe the work's context at the beginning of the session as the work is introduced to the rest of the group. The Tuning Protocol is a good example of such a process: Immediately after the general introduction, the presenter typically spends 5 minutes or so telling the group about the assignment, goals, criteria, and other aspects of the context for the work before the group begins to examine it. The Consultancy also begins with the presentation of contextual information about the presenter's dilemma.

Other protocols call for the context to be withheld initially. The group begins looking at the student work before any context is provided. In the Collaborative Assessment Conference, for example, the presenter shows the group the piece of student work but tells them nothing about it. Only in the second half of the protocol, after group members have thoroughly examined, described, and asked questions about the work, does the presenter tell them about the assignment, the grade level, who created the work, and how.

Why Is the Role of Context Important?

When educators first look at a piece of work, some of the first questions that spring to mind have to do with context. People naturally want to know about the assignment, the grade level, the background of the student, and so on. In a protocol that initially withholds that context, group members might feel frustrated at not being able to ask those questions. "Why should we guess about how old this student is or what he or she was trying to draw when the teacher can just tell us?" some people wonder. "That seems like a waste of time."

The answer is straightforward: Not knowing the context forces participants to look at the work more closely—without relying on preconceptions (or jumping to conclusions) about what a student of a certain age ought to be able to do, or how a certain kind of task ought to be responded to. It also gives the presenter the chance to hear fresh perspectives on students and their work. Often people who know neither the context nor the student will find in a piece of work evidence of important and powerful learning that presenters may miss because they are looking for something else or because they expect particular students to produce certain kinds of work.

Finally, withholding the context gives all the group's participants a chance to examine their own assumptions and preconceptions about how students carry out and convey meaning in their work. Many group members are surprised by one or several aspects of the context when it is revealed: The vivid artwork turns out to be the effort of a student whom they had never suspected of having artistic abilities; a student's reflection reveals that a research paper that seemed to the group to involve a lot of effort and care is in fact far less meaningful to the student than is the community service project that accompanied it. And so on.

As you consider choosing or designing a process for looking at student work, weigh carefully the role of context. The context you decide to share, and when you decide to share it, will have an impact on the kinds of issues and questions that arise. These subtle but powerful differences in approach and emphasis argue for careful, thoughtful, and repeated use of one protocol before moving on to others. As one district curriculum coordinator relates, "It takes three, four, five times with a protocol before the light goes on."

C H A P T E R   4

Three Ways of Looking Together at Student Work

IN THIS CHAPTER WE DESCRIBE three established structures for looking collaboratively at student work:

- The Tuning Protocol
- The Collaborative Assessment Conference
- The Consultancy

In Table 4.1 we give a quick overview of the key points of comparison and contrast between these three methods of looking at student work. A more detailed description and a bulleted agenda for each protocol follow.

You might use the following descriptions of the Tuning Protocol, the Collaborative Assessment Conference, and the Consultancy in several ways:

- If your group is in the early stages of deciding how to focus its efforts around looking at student work, you might try out one or more of these protocols in order to explore the opportunities provided by different formats.
- You might start with one of these models and alter or extend parts of it to better suit the goals of your particular group.
- You might use these protocols as models for developing your own unique protocol (as described in Chapter 5).

A word of caution: If most members of your group are novices at looking collaboratively at student work, you might want to begin by choosing one of these protocols and using it several times before modifying it or deciding to use a different one. These protocols are tools and, as with any

Table 4.1. Three Processes for Looking at Student Work

	Tuning Protocol	Collaborative Assessment Conference	The Consultancy
Purposes	• To develop more effective assignments, projects, and assessment tasks. • To develop common standards for students' work. • To support teachers' instructional practice through focusing on student performances and how they are assessed.	• To learn more about students' goals and interests: the problems and issues they choose to focus on in the course of an assignment. • To learn more about the strengths and needs of a particular student. • To reflect on and gather ideas for revising classroom practice.	• To gain insight into teachers' and administrators' dilemmas or "burning questions" arising from their practice. • To open up the thinking of the presenter and participants about problems of teaching and learning
Role of description, interpretation, and/or evaluation	*Primarily evaluation:* The process asks participants to provide warm and cool feedback on student work samples and teachers' assignments, scoring instruments, and so on.	*Primarily description, with some interpretation:* The process asks participants to describe the student work, to ask questions about it, and to speculate about the problems or issues in the work that the student was most focused on.	*Primarily interpretation:* The process asks participants to interpret the presenter's dilemma, to raise questions and offer hypotheses about the essence of that dilemma, and to offer other perspectives on the dilemma. Sometimes this interpretation may involve making observations (description) or suggestions (which may be interpreted as evaluative).
Presentation of the context for the student work	*Context presented initially:* At the beginning of the session, the presenting teacher typically provides descriptions of the assignment, scoring criteria, and so on.	*Context withheld until middle of process:* The presenting teacher does not describe the context for the work until after participants have looked carefully at it and formulated questions about it.	*Context presented initially:* The protocol begins with the presenting teacher's description of the dilemma and the context that gives rise to it.
Kinds and amount of student work typically shared	*Kinds of pieces:* Most often used for looking at work from a single assignment, task, or project. Samples of work usually include written and visual pieces, and sometimes a brief video as well. *Number of pieces:* Typically used with work from several students, often at different levels of accomplishment. May also be used with a single sample.	*Kinds of pieces:* Most often used to look at student work generated by an open-ended assignment (as opposed to worksheets). The work can come from any subject area (art, science, math, writing, and so on). *Number of pieces:* Usually one or two pieces of work from a single student. May also be used with multiple samples from a single student.	*Kinds of pieces:* Does not require student work samples; however, the presenter may choose to include them to illustrate the dilemma or ground it in the classroom context. *Number of pieces:* When student work is shared, the number of pieces varies from one to a few. The work might come from a single student or from several, depending on the dilemma that the presenter is trying to illustrate.

complex tool, they require practice in order for the user to gain the skill and comfort needed to derive the most benefit from them.

THE TUNING PROTOCOL: A DESCRIPTION

The Tuning Protocol was originally developed as a means for the five high schools in the Coalition of Essential Schools' Exhibitions Project to receive feedback from each other and fine-tune their developing student assessment systems, including exhibitions, portfolios, and design projects. Recognizing the challenges involved in developing new forms of assessment, the project staff, led by Joseph McDonald, developed a structure for facilitated discussions. The purpose of these discussions was to help teachers to share their students' work and their own work with colleagues and to reflect together on the lessons embedded there. Since its trial run in 1992, the Tuning Protocol has been widely used and adapted for professional development purposes in schools and within networks of teachers across the country.

To take part in the Tuning Protocol, teachers collect samples of their students' work on paper and, where possible, on video. They also gather the materials they themselves have created to support student performance, such as written descriptions of the assignment and scoring rubrics. In a circle of about 8 to 12 participants, usually other teachers, a facilitator leads the group through the protocol and keeps time. The presenter, or presenting team, describes the context for the student work (the task or project)— uninterrupted by questions or comments from participants.

Usually the presenter includes a focusing question about which he or she would especially welcome feedback, for example, "What evidence do you see of persuasive writing in the student work?" Participants have time to ask clarifying questions, which the presenter answers as concisely as possible. Next, the participants examine the samples of student work and other artifacts (the assignment, the rubric, and so on). Then, with the presenting teacher listening but silent, participants offer warm and cool feedback. Warm feedback comes from a deliberately supportive, appreciative perspective; it points to what is strong in the work (both the students' and the teacher's). Cool feedback comes from a deliberately questioning perspective; it refers to what may be missing or may need to be developed in the work. Participants often frame cool feedback as questions, for example, "How might the project be different if students chose their own research topics?"

After the feedback discussion, the presenter has the opportunity, again uninterrupted, to reflect briefly on the feedback and address any of the participants' comments or questions he or she chooses. Time is reserved for debriefing the group's experience of going through the protocol.

A schedule for a Tuning Protocol appears in Figure 4.1. The times provided on the schedule for the Tuning Protocol in Figure 4.1 are guidelines for facilitators. The facilitator and group may choose to condense or expand the times for individual steps to serve their needs. The overall schedule allows for a complete Tuning Protocol in about 50 minutes; however, if a group has more time, it may benefit from adding time to individual steps of the protocol, including a longer debrief discussion.

Guidelines for the Tuning Protocol

Participation in a structured process of professional collaboration such as this can be intimidating and anxiety producing, especially for the teacher presenting student work. Having a shared set of guidelines, or "norms," helps everybody participate in a manner that is respectful as well as conducive to constructive feedback. Below is one set of guidelines; your group may want to create its own. In any case, the group should go over the guidelines and the schedule before starting the protocol. The facilitator (or any participant) may refer to the guidelines as necessary during the protocol. A group may also want to revisit its guidelines in debriefing the protocol.

- Recognize the role of the presenter(s). By making their work more public, teachers are exposing themselves to kinds of feedback they may not be used to. Participants need to be thoughtful about how they phrase comments or questions. Inappropriate comments or questions should be reworded or withdrawn.
- Contribute to substantive discussion. Many teachers may be accustomed to blanket praise. Without thoughtful, probing cool questions and comments, they won't benefit from the Tuning Protocol experience.
- Recognize the role of the facilitator, particularly in regard to following the guidelines and keeping time. A Tuning Protocol that doesn't allow for all parts will do a disservice to the presenter and to the participants.

The Tuning Protocol in Action

Two high schools in neighboring districts on Long Island, New York, had been developing schoolwide goals for student performance. The principals considered how the two schools could become "critical friends" in helping each other address their goals. In conversation with members of their faculties and a researcher from Annenberg Institute at Brown University,

Figure 4.1. The Tuning Protocol

Developed by Joseph McDonald, Coalition of Essential Schools
Revised by David Allen

1. Introduction (5 minutes)
   - Facilitator briefly introduces protocol goals, guidelines, and schedule.
   - Participants briefly introduce themselves (if necessary).

2. Presentation (5–8 minutes)
   - Presenter shares the context for the student work, which might include information about the students, the class, the assignment or prompt, the learning goals (or standards) addressed, and/or the evaluation context (rubric, scoring criteria, and so on).
   - Presenting teacher frames a focusing question for feedback; facilitator may post focusing question for group to see.
   - Participants are silent; no questions are asked at this time.

3. Clarifying questions (5 minutes)
   - Participants ask "clarifying" questions in order to get information that may have been omitted in the presentation and which would help them understand the context for the student work.
   - The facilitator limits the questions to those that are truly "clarifying," determining which questions actually belong in the warm/cool feedback segment.

4. Examination of student work samples (10 minutes)
   - Participants look closely at the work samples—keeping the presenter's focusing question in mind, and perhaps taking notes for the warm and cool feedback.
   - Presenter is silent; participants do this work silently or talk quietly with a neighbor.

5. Pause to reflect on suitable comments and questions for warm and cool feedback (2–3 minutes)
   - Participants take a few minutes to reflect individually on what they would like to contribute to the feedback discussion.
   - Presenter is silent.

6. Warm and cool feedback (10–15 minutes)
   - Participants share feedback with one another while the presenter listens. The feedback typically begins with a few minutes of warm feedback, moves on to a few minutes of cool feedback, and then a mix of the two. *Warm feedback* points to strengths, for example, comments about how the work presented seems to meet the desired goals. *Cool feedback* identifies possible "disconnects," or gaps, between the work and the teacher's goals for it; cool feedback is often phrased as a question.
   - The facilitator may remind participants of the presenter's focusing question.
   - Presenter is silent; he or she may choose to take notes.

7. Reflection (5–10 minutes)
   - Presenter addresses those comments and questions he or she chooses to. The purpose is not to defend the student work or his or her own work, but instead to reflect aloud on those ideas or questions that seemed particularly compelling or intriguing.
   - Facilitator may intervene to help focus, clarify, and so on.
   - Participants listen silently.

8. Debrief (5–10 minutes)
   - Facilitator leads a reflection focused on the process, rather than content, of the discussion, that is, how the protocol supported a learning conversation.
   - Everyone participates.

they decided to use the Tuning Protocol as a way to help each of the schools connect its goals to classroom practice and student learning.

While the student performance goals for the schools varied somewhat, the principals were able to identify a small number of complementary goals on which to focus, including improving student writing across genres, improving oral communications skills, and developing and supporting an informed opinion. Each of the schools selected a group of 10–12 teachers from the science, math, and English departments to meet regularly to present and get feedback on projects and student work samples that reflect the goals.

The teachers met for a full day four times during the year, alternating between the two schools. In small-group discussions by discipline, a teacher, or team of teachers, presented a project and framed a focusing question that related to the schoolwide goal. Following the structure of the Tuning Protocol, the group asked clarifying questions, examined student work samples, and provided warm and cool feedback. Typically, each group went through two Tuning Protocols during the day with one presentation from each school.

In one meeting, a veteran science teacher presented his students' research projects. One of his school's goals for student performance was "developing and supporting an informed opinion." He began with the focusing question "How can a rubric that includes presentation skills be used as a teaching tool as well as an assessment instrument?" Participants viewed a video of a student presenting his research on conductivity and looked at the written outline for the presentation. In giving feedback, the teachers considered how students would benefit from viewing videotapes of prior presentations and discussing—even using—the rubric before they presented.

In his reflection, the presenting teacher recognized the value of the group's feedback, stating, "The protocol will have an immediate impact in my practice." Reflecting on comments from the protocol, he talked about showing students videotapes of prior performances and asking students to evaluate them and to discuss them using the rubric. "The rubric itself is not the teaching tool; it's a discussion tool." He also commented on the value of the Tuning Protocol structure: "I wouldn't have been able to hold back if not for the training of the Tuning Protocol, and so I wouldn't have heard the kinds of feedback I did."

The Tuning Protocol provided the structure for the conversation and helped keep the focus on student learning. After three sessions, teachers felt that there was a level of trust within the group and recognized that their conversations had begun to address core issues of teaching and learning, such as how goals for student performance can be brought to life in the projects students do and how the goals can be assessed in the work they produce.

THE COLLABORATIVE ASSESSMENT CONFERENCE: A DESCRIPTION

Since its development by Steve Seidel and colleagues at Harvard Project Zero in 1988, the Collaborative Assessment Conference has been used for various purposes: to hone participants' ability to look closely at and interpret students' work, to explore the strengths and needs of a particular child, to reflect on the work collected in student portfolios, and to foster conversations among faculty about the work students are doing and how to support that work. It provides a structure to help group members look together at a piece of work, first to determine what it reveals about the student and what that student is working on, and then to consider the implications of that student's work for teaching and learning in general. The structure for the conference has evolved from three key ideas:

- First, students use school assignments, especially open-ended ones, to tackle important problems that are of personal interest to them. Sometimes these problems are the same ones that the teacher has assigned them to work on, sometimes not. This means that a piece of student work has the potential to reveal not only the student's mastery of class goals, but also a wealth of information about the student, including his or her intellectual interests, strengths, and struggles.
- Second, adults can begin to see and understand the serious work that students undertake only if they suspend judgment long enough to look carefully and closely at what is actually in the work, rather than what they hope or expect to see in it.
- Third, teachers need the perspectives of others—especially those who are not familiar with their students or classroom contexts—in order to see the many facets that student's work may reveal and to help generate ideas about how to use this information to shape daily practice.

In Collaborative Assessment Conferences, the presenter brings a piece of student work to share with a group of 5 to 10 colleagues, usually other teachers and administrators. The protocol begins with the presenter showing, or distributing copies of, the piece to the group. Throughout the first part of the conference, the presenting teacher says nothing—giving no information about the student, the assignment, or the context in which the student worked.

Through a series of questions asked by the facilitator, such as "What do you see in the work?" the group members work to understand the piece by describing it in detail, raising questions about it, and speculating about the problems or issues in which the student was most engaged. They do this without making evaluations about the quality of the work or its appeal to their personal tastes. The facilitator helps this process by asking participants to identify evidence in the work for judgments, which inevitably slip out. For example, if someone comments that the work seems very creative, the facilitator might ask the participant to describe the aspect of the work that led him or her to say that.

In the second part of the conference, the focus broadens. Having concentrated intensively on the piece itself, the group, in conversation with the presenter, now considers the conditions under which the work was created as well as broader issues of teaching and learning. First, the presenter provides any information about the context for the work that he or she thinks is relevant. This might entail describing the assignment, responding to the discussion, answering questions raised in the first part of the conference (though the presenter can choose which of those questions to respond to), describing other work by the student, or commenting on how the presenter's own reading or observation of the work relates to that of the group.

Next, the facilitator asks the whole group (presenter included) to reflect on the ideas generated by the discussion of the piece. These might be reflections about specific next steps for the student in question, or ideas about what the participants might do in their own classes, or thoughts about teaching and learning in general. Finally, the whole group reflects on the conference itself.

Figure 4.2 is a working agenda for a Collaborative Assessment Conference. The time allotted for each step of the conference is not fixed, since the time needed for each step will vary according to the work being considered. At each stage, the facilitator makes the decision about when to move the group on to the next step. Typically, Collaborative Assessment Conferences take from 45 to 75 minutes.

The Collaborative Assessment Conference in Action

At an urban middle school in Massachusetts, teachers felt that they needed to "do more" with what students put into their folders. "I give the students time to reflect on their work, but I don't ever have time to reflect on it," said one teacher, to a chorus of head-nodding from others on the faculty.

Figure 4.2. Steps in the Collaborative Assessment Conference
Developed by Steve Seidel and Project Zero Colleagues

1. Getting started
    - The group chooses a facilitator who will make sure the group stays focused on the particular issue addressed in each step.
    - The presenting teacher puts the selected work in a place where everyone can see it or provides copies for the other participants. He or she says nothing about the work, the context in which it was created, or the student until Step 5.
    - The participants observe or read the work in silence, perhaps making brief notes about aspects of it that they particularly notice.

2. Describing the work
    - The facilitator asks the group, "What do you see?"
    - Group members respond without making interpretations, evaluations of the quality of the work, or statements of personal preference.
    - If evaluations or interpretations emerge, the facilitator asks the person to describe the evidence on which those comments are based.

3. Asking questions about the work
    - The facilitator asks the group, "What questions does this work raise for you?"
    - Group members state any questions they have about the work, the student, the assignment, the circumstances under which the work was carried out, and so on.
    - The presenting teacher makes notes about these questions (but does not answer them yet).

4. Speculating about what the student is working on
    - The facilitator asks the group, "What do you think the student is working on?"
    - Participants, drawing on their observation of the work, make suggestions about the problems or issues that the student focused on in carrying out the assignment.

5. Hearing from the presenting teacher
    - The facilitator invites the presenting teacher to speak.
    - The presenting teacher provides his or her perspective on the student's work, describing what he or she sees in it, responding to the questions raised, and adding any other information that he or she feels is important to share with the group.
    - The presenting teacher also comments on anything surprising or unexpected that he or she heard during the describing, questioning, and speculating phases.

6. Discussing implications for teaching and learning
    - The facilitator invites all participants, including the presenting teacher, to share any thoughts they have about their own teaching, children's learning, or ways to support this particular child in future instruction.

7. Reflecting on the Collaborative Assessment Conference
    - The group reflects together on their experiences of or reactions to the conference as a whole or particular parts of it.

8. Thanking the presenting teacher
    - The session concludes with acknowledgment of and thanks to the presenting teacher.

The school decided to institute regular Collaborative Assessment Conferences to give teachers more time to reflect on and discuss their students' work.

The school designated one of the weekly planning sessions each month to carrying out a Collaborative Assessment Conference. The teachers took turns bringing a piece, or pieces, of work from one of their students. To lead the meetings, the principal invited facilitators, from outside the school, who were well versed in the Collaborative Assessment Conference.

At first, the protocol felt awkward. Many teachers were uncomfortable with having to describe and ask questions about a piece of work without knowing the assignment or the context in which the student was working. "It would be a lot easier if we knew more about the assignment and the student," several teachers commented as they reflected on the session.

The presenting teachers were the first to identify the power of excluding context in the initial discussion. One remarked, "When people began asking questions about the work, like 'What did this student learn the most about while putting together this project?' I realized just how much I don't know about my students." She continued, "It gives me ideas for what I need to go back and talk with them about." Another teacher discovered that he never would have noticed the amount of effort and detail that went into a drawing that accompanied an essay without the benefit of other teachers' comments: "I was more focused on the writing part of the assignment. But as the other teachers described it, I started to see that the student had captured an important theme in that picture."

Over time, as the teachers became more comfortable with the Collaborative Assessment Conference, they found that the process helped them to identify important schoolwide concerns: how to balance supporting students in long-term projects with encouraging them to work independently, how to tie important curriculum topics to student interests, how to clarify for students standards and criteria for their work. These issues became topics for whole-school faculty meetings. One teacher summed up the importance of arriving at these issues through looking at student work:

> It's not like we couldn't have decided to concentrate on one of these issues without having gone through the Collaborative Assessment Conference. But, somehow, letting those issues grow out of looking at student work makes them feel more real, more grounded, more important. It's not someone telling us to pay attention to a particular issue. It's that we see the need for it ourselves in our students' work.

THE CONSULTANCY: A DESCRIPTION

The Consultancy (see Figure 4.3) was developed by Gene Thompson-Grove, Paula Evans, and Faith Dunne as part of the Coalition of Essential School's National School Re:Learning Faculty Program. It was further adapted and revised as part of the work of the National School Reform Faculty Project.

The goal of the Consultancy is to help participants gain insight into dilemmas or "burning questions" arising from their practice. The aim is less to solve a problem than it is to open up the thinking of the presenter and, thus, deepen the thinking of all participants. The Consultancy gives the presenter the chance to frame a question, respond to clarifying and probing questions, and then step back and listen to participants discuss the question from a variety of perspectives. It helps presenters to examine their assumptions about their own work, their students' work, and other aspects of their professional lives and often changes the way they think about an issue.

The presenter identifies a dilemma and hones a question related to this dilemma that he or she wants to bring to the group for their perspectives. Since the effectiveness of the Consultancy often depends on the quality of the presenter's question, developing an appropriate question is critical to the success of the protocol. The question should be one that focuses on the presenter's actions, behaviors, and beliefs, not on someone else's.

Framing a dilemma that is a true dilemma, rather than a question for which the presenter already has partial or full answers, is challenging. Facilitators often work closely with presenters before the protocol to frame an authentic dilemma that they think the group will be able to help with.

The presenter often brings a written description of the dilemma to the group in addition to any relevant samples of student work. The description ends with a question that gets at the heart of the dilemma and that guides the Consultancy group in its work. The Consultancy does not require that student work samples be used to illustrate the presenter's dilemma, but presenters often choose to include them. Sometimes the dilemma relates very directly to the student work samples that are presented; at other times, the samples serve to ground the dilemma in the reality of the classroom context.

After the presenter has given an overview of the dilemma and posed the question to the group, the participants ask clarifying questions. These are short-answer questions, such as "How many students are in your class?"

Next, the participants ask the presenter probing questions. The probing questions and the discussion that follows form the crux of the Consultancy. It may take some time for the group to learn the art of asking probing questions. As one facilitator emphasized, the Consultancy "lives

Figure 4.3. The Consultancy

Developed by Gene Thompson-Grove, Paula Evans, and Faith Dunne
Further revised by Gene Thompson-Grove and Colleagues in the
National School Reform Faculty Project

1. Presentation of the dilemma (5–10 minutes)

   The presenter gives an overview of the dilemma with which he or she is struggling and frames a question for the Consultancy group to consider. The framing of this question, as well as the quality of the presenter's reflection on his or her dilemma, are key features of this protocol. If the presenter has brought student work, educator work, or other artifacts, there is a pause here to silently examine the work or documents. The focus of the group's conversation is on the dilemma.

2. Clarifying questions (5 minutes)

   The group asks clarifying questions of the presenter—that is, questions that have brief, factual answers.

3. Probing questions (10 minutes)

   The group asks the presenter probing questions. These questions should be worded so that they help the presenter clarify and expand his or her thinking about the dilemma presented to the Consultancy group. The goal here is for the presenter to learn more about the question he or she has framed or to do some analysis of the dilemma presented. The presenter may respond to the group's questions, but the group does not discuss the presenter's responses. At the end of the 10 minutes, the facilitator asks the presenter to restate his or her question for the group.

4. Discussion of the dilemma (15 minutes)

   The group members talk with one another about the dilemma presented. Possible questions to frame the discussion include the following:

   - What did we hear?
   - What didn't we hear that we think might be relevant?
   - What assumptions seem to be operating?
   - What questions does the dilemma raise for us?
   - What do we think about the dilemma?
   - What might we do or try if faced with a similar dilemma? What have we done in similar situations?

   Members of the group sometimes suggest solutions to the dilemma. Most often, however, they work to define the issues more thoroughly and objectively. The presenter doesn't speak during this discussion, but instead listens and takes notes.

5. Presenter reflection (5 minutes)

   The presenter reflects on what he or she has heard and on what he or she is now thinking, sharing with the group anything that particularly resonated with him or her during any part of the Consultancy.

6. Debrief (5 minutes)

   Everyone participates as the facilitator leads a brief conversation about the protocol.

in the probing questions. It takes practice. . . . Becoming good at probing questions is the role of participants." Other facilitators concur that the probing-question step can be the most challenging. One commented:

> The trick is finding the right amount of cognitive dissonance to cause. After all, the point of the consultancy is to shake up how we see our own dilemmas—to cause cognitive dissonance—but not to cause so much that we shut down or get overwhelmed.

After asking the probing questions, the Consultancy group discusses the presenter's focusing question. The presenter, who may choose to push his or her chair back from the circle, listens as the group wrestles with the question he or she has raised. "You can almost see the presenter's world opening up," reports one teacher. "It helps the presenter realize, perhaps for the first time, that there were presuppositions or areas that [he or] she never thought about before."

The Consultancy in Action

A school in Massachusetts for Grades 7–12, whose principal is an experienced facilitator of "critical friends groups," uses the Consultancy when a teacher has a burning question or dilemma. The critical-friends groups, teams of a dozen teachers of diverse grades and subjects, meet monthly to discuss issues of teaching and learning in their school. Although the meetings are scheduled a year in advance, the teachers do not sign up in advance to present their cases. Instead, the critical-friends-group facilitators visit each class during the month to find out which teachers might have a burning question for the group. The facilitators also weed out questions that are inappropriate for the Consultancy.

One month a new teacher formulated a question. He wondered how effort was factored into the assessment equation in a school that focused on written assessments. When it came to effort, he thought—echoing the Supreme Court justice's infamous remark about pornography—"teachers know it when they see it." He knew he was including his interpretation of the child's effort in his evaluation—even though it was not on the rubric he shared with his students. He was concerned that he was assessing effort—how hard his students were working—without really telling them. Through this first step of the Consultancy, a clear dilemma emerged: "What does effort look like?" The facilitator reminded the group members that their job was not to solve the presenter's problem; rather, it was to open up the presenter's thinking. In doing so, they themselves would doubtless come away "knowing something new."

After an initial discussion of the question, the group members decided to postpone the remainder of the Consultancy until they could gather more data. They visited the teacher's class and wrote down what they considered to be student effort. After gathering evidence on the question, the group reconvened to share notes. The new question was "How much does effort factor into an assessment when effort is not in the rubric?"

Next, the Consultancy group asked probing questions. These questions tested the assumptions of the presenter. It emerged, for example, that the presenter assumed that a student listening to an iPod during a writing assignment was automatically putting in less effort. The evidence from the classroom observations raised the possibility that listening to an iPod did not necessarily mean that a student was not trying.

As a result of listening to the Consultancy group's subsequent discussion, the presenting teacher realized that he had to include in the rubric more about the students' process. He had to be more open with the students about the role of effort in his assessment. As for the group, one teacher commented: "We each realized we made assumptions about what effort kids were making. We learned what effort looked like."

In the final step of debriefing the protocol, the facilitator allowed the presenting teacher to make a few general comments and then asked him questions that were more focused: "What question was most intriguing? What did you hear that made you uncomfortable? Where was the greatest dissonance?" The group members then discussed their experiences during the protocol, in particular, how it had supported or constrained their conversation. In thinking about the role of the Consultancy Protocol, the facilitator said:

> The Consultancy is a very beautifully choreographed piece. If any one of the steps is done carelessly, it does not hold together. All of the steps are important. Trust each step. You never know which step will be critical to the presenter.

Over the years, facilitators and teacher groups in this school have become attuned to what the principal calls the "reciprocity of how the protocols talk to each other." Sometimes a Collaborative Assessment Conference leads to a dilemma, and then the Consultancy becomes the logical next protocol to use. As teachers become more at ease with the structure and nuances of the protocols, they begin using them as the need arises. At the beginning of the school year they use the Tuning Protocol to fine-tune units of curriculum with parents and students. Informally, during the year, teachers use the Tuning Protocol for lessons they are about to teach. They show newly developed lesson plans to colleagues to get quick warm and cool feedback.

Like the other two protocols, the Consultancy provides a solid structure as an aid for looking together at student work, in this case by focusing the group's conversation on the presenter's dilemma about that work. The dilemmas and questions provide infinite variety within the structure. A seasoned facilitator has learned the importance of emphasizing to groups the purpose of the Consultancy:

> The purpose of the structure is not to hammer out a solution to a problem. From the beginning, the mindset of problem solving has to be put on a ledge. What we're trying to do is help the presenter to get into the state of dialogue, the free flow of ideas, without judgment, which opens up the presenter's thinking. We help the presenter get out of her own way and examine her assumptions and in so doing, we learn something new.

C H A P T E R 5

Three Schools That Developed Their Own Protocols

WITH EACH PASSING YEAR comes the appearance of more and more protocols and resources for looking at student work collaboratively. Yet chances are good that, to achieve your and your school's particular goals, you may need to adapt existing protocols or develop new ones. This chapter contains examples of three schools that did exactly that:

- A middle school that developed a training protocol to prepare judges of student exhibitions
- An elementary school that created a new protocol for parent-student-teacher conferences
- A high school that adapted the Tuning Protocol, creating its own protocol, which teachers could use to give one another feedback on writing assignments

With specific goals in mind, the teachers and administrators set out to shape their own processes for examining and discussing student work. Their stories offer examples of protocols that were developed in response to specific needs and for specific contexts (in contrast to the models in Chapter 4, which were designed for more general use). Each example is presented in five parts, mirroring the steps described in Chapter 2:

- Taking stock of current ways of looking at student work
- Establishing goals and framing questions
- Choosing, adapting, or developing a protocol for looking collaboratively at student work
- Using the protocol over the course of several meetings
- Periodically reflecting on the goals and framing questions and revising how the group is using the protocol to address those goals and questions.

BRINGING OUTSIDERS IN: USING STUDENT WORK
TO TRAIN EXHIBITION JUDGES

In the spring, the Exhibition Committee at Rosemont Middle School faced a knotty problem. Like the faculties of the other two ATLAS schools* in Norfolk, Virginia, the faculty of Rosemont had committed itself to holding public student exhibitions that used "outside" judges—people from outside the school who would sit on panels with Rosemont teachers to assess the students' presentations. Rosemont's Exhibition Committee, composed of several faculty members and an administrator, anticipated that there would be many concerns about this plan—from teachers, parents, students, and the prospective judges themselves. The committee's main concern, however, was helping community members who would be serving as judges to carry out their roles in a way that would ensure the best possible learning experience for all the students.

Taking Stock

Student exhibitions, made up of research papers and oral presentations, had been instituted the previous year and had proved to be a daunting challenge for both the students and the faculty. Even though the faculty had been reshaping the curriculum to include more performance-oriented and hands-on activities, the students still struggled with the unfamiliar tasks of researching and managing long-term projects. A new and time-consuming mentoring system, whereby groups of two to six students were paired with each teacher, staff member, and administrator in the school, presented stubborn organizational problems that the entire staff wrestled with over the course of the year.

Ultimately, to keep students from being penalized by the inevitable glitches in the new system, the school decided not to have students present their exhibitions to a public panel at the end of that 1st year. Rather, teachers at all grade levels were encouraged to help their students to carry out

*ATLAS Communities is a comprehensive school improvement initiative designed to help create high-performing schools that serve all students well. ATLAS Communities began as a collaboration among four organizations (the Coalition of Essential Schools at Brown University; Education Development Center, in Newton, Massachusetts; Project Zero at Harvard University; and the School Development Program at Yale University) and three school systems (Gorham, Maine; Norfolk, Virginia; and Prince George's County, Maryland). For more information, see http://www.atlascommunities.org.

projects related to the topics and issues already studied in the curriculum. Twenty students were asked to present their work to an audience of students, parents, teachers, and other adults. Although the audience members were allowed to ask questions of the student presenters, no formal assessment of their work was made, since the classroom teachers had already assigned the students grades for their work.

At the beginning of the 2nd year of exhibitions, however, the faculty felt ready to take the next step: turning the public exhibitions into occasions for assessment and evaluation. Everyone agreed that this aspect of the exhibition presentation was important. But the idea of inviting outsiders in to play such a critical role raised several concerns for Rosemont's staff.

Some were troubled by the prospect of exposing students' work to the scrutiny of people who might not understand what to expect of middle school students. "If the outside judges don't know our students or where they started or what we teach or how we teach it, how can they judge the work fairly?" wondered one teacher. An administrator pointed out that the process was likely to be as uncomfortable for teachers as it was for students, since looking at the students' work was like "holding up a mirror" to the teachers' work. Given that teaching had until recent years been a solitary undertaking at the school, and given that the whole idea of supporting exhibitions in the classrooms was still new, people were not sure what to expect once they invited virtual strangers to peer more closely into that mirror.

Jane Montagna, a member of Rosemont's Exhibition Committee and the staff developer for the school, had another worry. Earlier in the year, she, along with members of the exhibition committees of all three ATLAS schools in Norfolk, had participated in a modified Tuning Protocol session facilitated by ATLAS staff members who were visiting the schools. In that session, they had looked at videotapes of student exhibitions and discussed the quality of the students' work.

After that session, Jane had conducted similar meetings for Rosemont's teachers. The meetings focused on reviewing samples from the previous year's student exhibitions. The goal, as she saw it, was to help teachers think about the purposes of exhibitions and how to help students build the skills that were necessary for carrying them out. In discussions in these meetings, she had discovered a sharp divide: Some believed that the most important aspect of an exhibition at this level was the degree to which it supported students' self-esteem. Others thought that the primary purpose of the exhibition was to push students to think more deeply about the issue they had studied. She realized that this was bound to be a critical point for all who would be serving as judges for the exhibitions—the people from outside the school as well as the teachers.

Establishing Goals and Framing Questions

To address these worries and to ensure that the exhibition experience would be a good one for both the students and the panel judges, the Exhibition Committee knew that some initial training of the prospective judges was needed. With Jane taking the lead, the committee settled on two goals for the training session:

- To help judges develop an appreciation of Rosemont's goals for student exhibitions as a vehicle for deepening students' understanding of a topic
- To raise the judges' awareness about the role of personal experience and bias in exhibition judging

Jane explained the first goal:

It's not just about asking the easy questions that make the kids feel good because they can give an answer. And it's not just about who can give the smoothest presentation. We really want people to question the kids in a way that gets at the kids' understanding.

The second goal grew out of the committee's recognition that people see the judge's role in very different ways. The members of the committee did not want to suggest that one definition of the judge's role was the "right" one. However, they did want to give the judges the opportunity to think about and discuss with others their own understanding of the role of judge and how their personal experiences might affect their judgments.

Developing a Protocol

It didn't take long for the committee to decide that the best way to prepare people for looking at student work was to spend the training session looking at and discussing student exhibitions that were similar to the ones the "trainees" would encounter as judges. In consultation with the Exhibition Committee, the staff developers at the other ATLAS schools, and the researchers from the ATLAS project, Jane designed the core of the "Judges Training Session": having the participants watch videos of two brief student exhibitions and then address some questions about each. The questions were aimed at getting people to think in concrete ways about the two goals for the session.

The agenda for the session is reproduced below. In practice, Items 2 through 6 constitute a protocol for viewing and discussing videotaped samples of the student work. The last item offers participants an opportunity to debrief their protocol-guided discussion:

AGENDA FOR JUDGES' TRAINING

1. Welcome and presentation of goals.
2. Small-group discussions in which each person in the group answers the question "What is the role of a judge?" (Group spokesperson reports the small group's discussion to the large group.)
3. Viewing of first videotape of a student exhibition. (The tape is stopped just before the judges on the tape begin asking questions of the student.)
4. Whole-group discussion of the question "If you were the judge, what questions would you ask this student?" (Group discusses the question, and then watches the actual questioning session on tape and compares their questions.)
5. Viewing of second videotape of a student exhibition.
6. Whole-group discussion of the questions "How did you feel as you watched the tape? What do you think the judges did well (or not)?"
7. Brief description of developmental issues of middle school children.
8. Questions and concerns.

Using the Protocol

On the day of the training, 20 prospective judges assembled in the middle school's library to reflect on the purposes of exhibitions and the role of judge. The group consisted of administrators from the district office, staff from the district attorney's office and the district attorney, parents, high school teachers, high school students, and a few middle school teachers. Jane introduced the goals and agenda for the training and then led the group through the various steps.

In the initial discussion of the role of judge, most members of the group gave similar responses. However, differences in points of view began to emerge as the group discussed the specific student exhibitions they had watched on the videotape, especially after they had watched the second one. The first video clip had depicted a confident and well-prepared student who gave her presentation smoothly and responded to her judges' questions quickly and thoughtfully. In the second video clip, however, the presenting student appeared to struggle more. Her presentation, which she appeared to have memorized, was recited in a low tone of voice and almost mechanically. When the videotape showed the judges asking her questions, the student was often silent for a period, furrowing her brow and twisting her hands behind her as she tried to think of answers. Her answers were often halting.

Jane posed the questions outlined in Item 6: "How did you feel as you watched the tape? What do you think the judges did well?" One participant responded, "I thought the judges' questions created too many negative experiences for that child. They kept asking questions at a higher level, instead of easing up when they saw she couldn't handle it. I felt terrible watching it. I felt like I wanted to get out of there for her." "I had those feelings, too," responded another participant, "but if we don't have some questions of a probing nature, we're negating the whole purpose of what the students are doing. And we need to allow them time to think."

Another participant returned to the issue of how to make the presenter comfortable: "The judges [on the videotape] should have started with a less challenging question when they saw how nervous she was." A fourth participant pointed out that, in fact, no more than 12 seconds elapsed between the time a question was asked and the time the student answered. "I started timing when I saw how much time she was taking," this participant announced. "And she always came up with an answer," another offered, "It just took her longer than we were comfortable with."

The debate was not resolved in favor of one questioning approach or another, but the participants' reflections at the end of the session revealed that collaboratively examining the student's work had given them some valuable strategies, which they could use when serving on their own panels. "I realized the importance of the nonverbal communication. It's important to be able to read body language in order to help the student do her best. If a student looks really uncomfortable, I want to be sure to give her a little more support, like an encouraging nod or a smile."

One participant commented that the question period seemed to reveal much more about what the student understood than the presentation did: "Obviously, [the student in the video] knew much more than she stated in her presentation. Only the questions got that knowledge out of her." Another agreed: "I want to be very careful about how I ask questions—it's hard to walk that line between making the child feel comfortable so she can do her best and finding out what she really knows."

Reflecting on the Protocol

The next day the public exhibitions began. Over the course of the week, both the strengths and the weaknesses of the training session emerged. The experience of looking at student exhibitions on videotape proved valuable. According to one participant, "It was extremely helpful to see what an exhibition looked like before I had to judge one—even seeing one in which the judges were not very good. At least it told me what I didn't want to do." Another commented, "I'm glad I got to hear what other people thought about the same presentation. It made me realize that there's no right way to be a judge."

Judges, as well as teachers not involved in the judging process, voiced concern over the lack of common standards for assessing the students' work. While all the participants felt prepared for the question-and-answer period, they had not had time to practice actually scoring presentations and papers. Several mentioned that more practice scoring student work and comparing results might have helped with this issue. Others pointed out that clearer criteria for the student performances would have helped.

A final concern emerged about panels on which all the judges adopted the same approach to the role, so that all were either wholehearted supporters or critical questioners, creating an unchallenging experience for students in the first case and a too-challenging one for them in the second. Jane reflected that given a little more time, the training session might have enabled her to size up the preferred approaches of individual judges and to create more balanced panels—panels that included both judges who "pushed" and judges who "comforted." "Good ideas for next year," Jane pointed out.

PARENT-STUDENT-TEACHER CONFERENCES: LOOKING AT STUDENT WORK FROM MULTIPLE PERSPECTIVES

The faculty of the Charles Shaw Middle School in Gorham, Maine, wanted to fine-tune its assessment system. They wanted students to take more responsibility for their learning. They also wanted to allow for more individualized attention, for more parent participation, and for a continuing focus on looking at and discussing the things that students do and make.

Taking Stock

Alternative assessment strategies had long been part of the Gorham school district's approach to education when it became a member of ATLAS Communities. Students in every school in the district kept portfolios; gave periodic "benchmark exhibitions"; and carried out mandatory written and oral performances, which were assessed with criteria common to all the schools. In addition, years earlier, when the staff had initiated portfolio work, they had begun using Collaborative Assessment Conferences as a way to help teachers talk together about student work. (See Chapter 4 for a description of the Collaborative Assessment Conference.)

Teachers and administrators, though, were not entirely satisfied with the assessment system. At Shaw Middle School, teachers and administrators tried to pinpoint this dissatisfaction in reflections at staff meetings. Eventually, they identified three problems in their current methods of assessing student work:

- Open houses and parent conferences, which mainly focused on report cards, did not provide parents with an in-depth opportunity for learning about student goals and performances.
- Students did not have specific personal goals for which they felt accountable. Nor did they understand the standards or criteria by which their work was being evaluated.
- Forging alliances with parents to foster the education of their children was difficult when parents did not understand the goals for their children and had no chance to examine their children's work in order to see how they were achieving those goals.

Establishing Goals and Framing Questions

On the basis of these concerns, the Shaw staff articulated the specific goals that they wanted to achieve with a new way of looking at student work:

- To increase communication among parents, teachers, and students
- To delineate the different responsibilities of parents, teachers, and students in the student's education
- To link student performances to specific individualized and personal goals for each student and to use those performances to gauge how well the goals were being met
- To discuss meaningful interventions to foster continued growth and development for each student

Developing a Protocol

Shaw Middle School's School Planning and Management Team, an advisory body composed of teachers, administrators, parents, community members, and students, began to explore ways of making the assessment system more meaningful for students and teachers. Drawing on the teachers' experiences with the Collaborative Assessment Conference, the School Planning and Management Team began considering the possibility of developing a parent-student-teacher conference that would enable parents, their children, and teachers to look at and discuss the children's work on a regular basis.

After much debate, the members of the School Planning and Management Team decided to include students in the traditional parent-teacher conferences. They also decided that the major activity of those conferences would be looking at and discussing pieces of student work and that the students themselves would take the major responsibility for organizing and running the conference. The School Planning and Management Team presented the idea to the Shaw faculty, who worked out the details of implementation. A year later, the district endorsed the idea of parent-student-teacher conferences and set aside time for such conferences in all schools at designated points throughout the school year, extending the school calendar to create time for the conferences and adding staff development to help teachers prepare for them.

The original implementation plan developed by the faculty involved holding conferences twice a year; 3 days in September and 3 days in March were devoted to half-hour-long conferences with each student and her or his parents or guardians. Both conferences centered on examining and discussing the work that the student presented. In the September conference known as the "entry conference," teachers, parents, and students reviewed work to help the students set personal goals for their learning for the year. The later conference gave everyone a chance to examine students' work for evidence of progress toward those goals.

PARENT-STUDENT-TEACHER CONFERENCE: BEGINNING OF THE YEAR

1. Teacher reviews with parent and student the purposes of the entry conference: establishing learning goals for the school year.
2. Student shares with teacher and parent the one or two pieces of work that he or she has selected from last year's portfolio and explains the strengths and weaknesses he or she feels they demonstrate. Teacher and parent offer comments after the student has commented.
3. Student identifies the learning goals that that he or she wants to concentrate on this year. Parent and teacher help refine the goals.
4. Student, parent, and teacher develop an action plan: steps that can

be taken by all three of them at home and at school to support the student in achieving his or her learning goals.

Using the Protocol

Recognizing that this approach differed significantly from what parents and students were used to, the faculty at Shaw took steps to prepare themselves, as well as students and parents, for the conferences. Before the start of school in the fall, teachers participated in staff development activities that helped them explore ways of setting individual student goals with students and parents. They also considered various formats for the entry conference meeting in September. During these sessions, they worked in small groups and, using actual pieces of student work, role-played different scenarios. They practiced explaining the rationale for such conferences to students and parents and, in the process, discussed many of their own concerns and reservations about the new approach.

During the initial weeks of school, teachers and students considered various ways of documenting the students' work and progress. The teachers reminded students that their portfolios were not collections of "best works," but rather an accumulation of pieces of work that showed their growth in knowledge or skills. Initial drafts, revisions, completed works, and their own reflections on their work could all provide evidence of that growth.

Teachers also discussed with students the goal-setting that students and teachers carry out. They explained the rationale for goal-setting, distinguished between long- and short-range goals, discussed obstacles to reaching them, and emphasized the need for periodic "check-ins" to monitor and assess progress. Some teachers asked students to discuss their preliminary goals at home with their parents so that the first conference could focus on refining the goals and discussing how to reach them.

Before the first conference, teachers sent a letter home to parents explaining the aims and organization of the parent-student-teacher conference. Some teachers included with the letter a list of questions that the parents and students could discuss together before the conference, such as "When do I learn best?" and "What do I want my teacher to know about me?"

The students took responsibility for establishing the focus of the parent-student-teacher conference. They selected one or two pieces of their work to present at the conference, pieces that they felt represented both some of their strengths and the areas in which they wanted to improve. After considering the work, student, parent, and teacher concentrated on articulating goals and developing action plans that would help the student to work toward them, both at school and at home. The conversations were led by students, with the teachers serving as facilitators. As one teacher explained:

> A major student goal might be "I want to get better organized." My challenge is to become a good facilitator and ask, "Laurie, what do you mean by that? How will we know if you are better organized when we get together again? What can you do to prove that you are better organized?"

Reflecting on the Protocol

Drawing on their strong tradition of reflective practice, the Shaw teachers stopped to ponder what they were learning at every step of the way during the implementation process. They wrote personal reflections during staff development meetings; they discussed their preparation for the conferences as well as the conferences themselves during regular team meetings; they sent out questionnaires to parents and analyzed and distributed the results. Through these reflections, the faculty were able to identify many strengths in the parent-student-teacher conferences as they had been designed:

- *Preconference organization and preparation.* The faculty felt that their attention to this area had been energy well spent. As one teacher pointed out, "People really need support whenever they try something new, and particularly when the extended community is invited to become actively involved."
- *Focus on actual pieces of student work and their connection to specific goals.* The faculty agreed that their initial focus on the connection between goals and student performances was important and should continue to be emphasized. Many also cited the importance of having the actual work at the center of the conversation. One teacher explained, "With the portfolio on the table, it was easy to convey to parents the reason for poor performances—a reason based not on ability but on certain choices made by the student."
- *Student involvement.* Most of the faculty were pleased with the active role students played in the parent-student-teacher conference. Parents showed great pride as they watched their children assume ownership of their work and participate in the conversations. In addition, many teachers felt the "burden of proof" shift from their shoulders to the students':

  > The parent-student-teacher conference was the easiest conference I've ever had. It was not incumbent on me to take

responsibility for defining the progress the student had made. I was an observer in the process that involved meaningful conversation focused on student work. The onus was on the child to talk about her own work intelligently and confidently, to describe what she had learned and how she would use that learning in the future.

- *Parent involvement.* After the initial conference, the staff at Shaw polled parents on the effectiveness of various aspects of the conference. More than 70% of the parents who responded to the poll rated as "very helpful" (the highest rating) the conference's focus on their child as a learner, the process of setting goals with their child and the child's teacher, and their child's participation in the conference. For the teachers, the parent-student-teacher conferences become another way to invite parents to support the education of their children.
- *Administrative support.* Many teachers acknowledged the central role that the administration had played in nurturing the success of the first round of parent-student-teacher conferences. With such encouragement, teachers felt free to take the risks required to launch a new assessment system. As one teacher noted, "It's critical to have a supportive administration that recognizes that this process will not be flawless."

The faculty's reflection also generated several points for improvement in future parent-student-teacher conferences. First, they expanded the time allotted for the August in-service professional development dedicated to preparing for the conferences. The extra time allowed them to address in more depth the key elements of the initial parent-student-teacher conference and the things each conference participant needs to do in order to prepare for it.

Second, they realized that September was too early in the year for students to formulate goals. They proposed that at the end of the year, students select several pieces of work from their portfolios to carry with them to next year's class. Then, when students were asked to draft goals at the beginning of the year, they would have a more substantive body of work to refer to. The teachers also recommended to the district that the 6 conference days be reallocated. Instead of 3 entry conference days in the fall and 3 final conference days in the spring, they proposed three periods of 2 days each, thus providing a midyear check-in conference.

Finally, the teachers suggested several steps to further encourage both parents and students to take active roles in the students' learning and assessment:

- Invite parents to a forum in the fall to explain the rationale for the parent-student-teacher conference.
- Make sure the letter sent ahead to parents passes the "kitchen table test," in other words, that it is clear and free of education jargon.
- Create more opportunities (in addition to the parent-student-teacher conference) for students to share and celebrate their work.

While all agreed that bringing parents, students, and teachers together to look at student work took a degree of organization, energy, and time not required by the more traditional conferences, many teachers also acknowledged the added meaning and value it had brought to the assessment system. One teacher summed it up:

> Good teachers have always looked thoughtfully at student work. We've used formative and summative evaluations and in-class conferencing. We've always looked at student work and hoped we would target improvement in the next learning experience. With the parent-student-teacher conference, we've taken that process to a new, collaborative level. We've come to recognize what little value there is in just slapping an A or a D on student work. Goals emerge through . . . reflection on and discussion of that work. Assessment is no longer an isolated, one-shot deal.

DEVELOPING A SCHOOLWIDE FOCUS ON WRITING

Park East High School, a small public school in East Harlem, New York City, had been a school that primarily served students who had experienced failure in other city high schools. Nick Mazzarella, the school's new principal, wanted to transform it into a college-preparatory high school that students and their families would choose to attend directly after junior high school. To help achieve this goal, he drew on the school's existing partnership with the Institute for Student Achievement (ISA), a nonprofit organization that supports the development of small public high schools.* At that

---

*The Institute for Student Achievement, a nonprofit school redesign organization based in Lake Success, New York, works with school districts to create small public high schools and convert large high schools into small learning communities that serve students at risk of failure. ISA's goal is to help these small schools and small learning communities graduate all students prepared for success in college and work. For more information, see http://www.studentachievement .org.

time, ISA was introducing a new model for whole-school change, drawing on a set of research-based principles.

As an ISA partner school, Park East began to work with Suzy Ort as its school coach and participated in ongoing performance assessments in math and writing administered by ISA's partner organization, the National Center for Restructuring Education, Schools, and Teaching (NCREST), at Teachers College, Columbia University. The results of the first performance assessments along with other evidence pointed to one of the school's most daunting challenges: helping students who entered the school with very poor literacy skills to become proficient writers.

Taking Stock

Through the school's collaboration with ISA, several Park East teachers had participated in the scoring conferences sponsored by ISA. These scoring conferences brought together teachers from different disciplines in ISA partner schools, their school coaches, and NCREST staff to score the students' writing samples from performance assessments in writing that were administered in the fall and spring of each year. At each scoring conference, participants began by meeting in small groups to analyze the writing prompt that students were given, look closely at the scoring rubric, and then score sample papers using the rubric. Through sharing their scores and the rationales behind them, participants learned to use rubrics to assess student writing. During Park East's regular whole-faculty professional development sessions, the teachers who had attended these scoring conferences had mentioned some of the techniques they had learned, and their ideas had sparked the interest of other faculty members.

Establishing Goals and Framing Questions

School coach Suzy Ort and the newly formed faculty-led Professional Development Committee took note of this enthusiasm. The committee members had been searching for ways to help the whole faculty meet the established schoolwide goal of supporting literacy across the curriculum. In committee discussions, the members had already agreed that finding a way to have faculty share both their writing assignments and their students' work would be a powerful way of enhancing how literacy was supported in all the subject areas. But this was a daunting undertaking in a school in which faculty members had rarely shared actual examples of teaching and learning from their own classrooms. Could they adapt the scoring-conference protocol to help the whole faculty gain experience in examining and evaluating student writing? This could serve as an initial step toward eventually sharing and giving feedback on one another's assignments.

The committee knew they had two important assets to work with: The school's weekly 50-minute whole-faculty professional development session would provide them with the time they needed to try out the modified scoring conference, and the teachers who had already been through a scoring conference could lend their experience to ensure that the modified version ran smoothly. The last puzzle—where to get the student writing samples—was solved when they decided to use a subset of the Park East students' responses to the performance assessments collected by ISA and NCREST.

Developing a Protocol

Suzy obtained a set of Park East student work from the fall ISA writing assessment, which demonstrated a range of levels according to the scoring rubric (from "insufficient" to "competent"). In January at a whole-faculty professional development session, teachers read the prompt, which instructed the students to write a persuasive essay or letter on a controversial issue. Then they brainstormed what a high-quality student response would look like and familiarized themselves with the scoring rubric, which included a holistic score from "insufficient" to "skillful," as well as scores on main point, support, organization, language use/style, and conventions. Then each participant read and scored three to five samples from Park East students.

In the small-group discussions that followed, teachers were able to identify strengths in the student writing but also significant weaknesses in how students organized and supported their positions. Specifically, teachers commented that they noticed that, in general, mechanics, or "conventions," in the rubric's terminology, did not pose as much of a problem as they had expected. Rather, the teachers saw that for the most part students were able to identify a clear main point and write competently with relatively few errors. However, only rarely were students able to elaborate on arguments or deploy evidence in support of a position they had taken.

The Professional Development Committee planned two follow-up sessions for February. In one, teachers discussed different ways of giving feedback to students on their writing, including using rubrics, editing marks, model papers, and narrative comments from teachers. They discussed how such strategies might be employed to support the students whose papers they had read in the previous session.

In the second session, teachers met in subject departments to discuss the writing opportunities they provided for students within their individual classes. They reviewed a long list of possible writing activities created by the coach and members of the Professional Development Committee, from lists and recipes, to oral histories and poems, to research papers. They identified those they had already used as well as some they might try. Facilitators asked the teachers to consider presenting both an assignment that included writing and the student work that was done in response to the assignment at a future professional development meeting.

In the next session, the coach and the Professional Development Committee decided to take the step of having the faculty look at and give feedback on a teacher's assignment and the student writing that it generated. They decided that the Tuning Protocol would provide a good introduction to this kind of work and invited a staff member from NCREST to facilitate a Tuning Protocol for the whole faculty. Lisa Purcell, a social studies teacher, agreed to present a research project on world religions. She shared the initial assignment she had given to students, several different samples of the research papers students had done, and the rubric she had used to assess their work. For most of the teachers at Park East, this Tuning Protocol served as their introduction to using a protocol to look at a colleague's assignment and student work samples and offer critical feedback.

The Professional Development Committee reflected on the whole-faculty Tuning Protocol. In written evaluations and informal comments, most teachers gave the professional development session high marks: "Brave," and "ambitious," they wrote. Overall the teachers seemed mostly to appreciate the relatively in-depth look into the thinking behind the creation and careful execution of a writing assignment. They were impressed by their colleague's willingness to make public her work and that of her students and expressed strong interest in doing this kind of professional development again.

The committee agreed that this form of professional development should continue. Now the question became, how could the work expand so that more teachers could present their assignments and get feedback from colleagues, given the limited amount of time dedicated to whole-faculty professional development? In collaboration with the Professional Development Committee, Suzy developed the "Park East Protocol," an adaptation of the Tuning Protocol that could be completed in about 20 minutes, which would allow three teachers to present in an hour-long professional development session. To help set an easy tone for the discussions, Suzy was conscious of making the language of the protocol informal and inviting rather than formal and academic.

PARK EAST PROTOCOL

(approx. 20 minutes)

1. Presenter intros what they did, what they hoped to accomplish and how it went. Poses focusing question if they have a burning one, otherwise asks for general feedback/thinking
2. BRIEF clarifying questions (don't get hung up here)
3. Quiet reading of the assignment and one example of student work
4. Small group members give WARM feedback about what they appreciated about the work, what was particularly interesting or strong, etc.
5. Small group members give COOL feedback, i.e.: what lingering questions do you have, additional ideas/suggestions, etc.
6. PRESENTER IS SILENT DURING FEEDBACK TIME
7. Presenter reflects on what they've heard, what sounded useful, provoked their thinking etc. . . . . presenters respond only to the feedback they want to respond to. (They drive this boat.)

Using the Protocol

In the first professional development session in which the new Park East Protocol was used, three teachers from different disciplines (math, health, and social studies) presented assignments and samples of student writing. The committee had designed the agenda so that all teachers who were not presenting in one of the 20-minute slots would rotate as a group, enabling each group to experience each of the three presentations during the three 20-minute blocks. Members of the Professional Development Committee tightly facilitated the small groups to keep them on schedule.

In their written evaluations of the sessions, teachers commented that despite the breakneck speed of the presentations, they loved the extremely rare opportunity of seeing "live" examples of assignments being used in different classrooms in the school. For some, the frenetic pace made the endeavor feel "safe," because there was not much time to delve into extensive commentary on the quality of the teachers' work. It was viewed by teachers as an introduction to the kinds of writing assignments that were currently being used as well as an opportunity to provide quick feedback to the teacher.

Based on the success of the trial run for the Park East Protocol, the three-protocol format was repeated in the following professional development session with three more teachers presenting and getting feedback from colleagues. At the end of the school year, as teachers formally reflected on the sessions that the Professional Development Committee had organized over the course of the year, those involving the Park East Protocol were mentioned repeatedly as the year's most interesting and worthwhile sessions, because of their practicality—teachers began to adopt and adapt each other's practices—and because the sessions provided an opportunity to discuss the quality of student writing. In the following school year, they became a regular feature of weekly professional development meetings.

Reflecting on the Protocol

Through this gradually expanding use of protocols, which began with looking at Park East student work in response to a prompt from the ISA writing performance assessment, nearly half the teachers presented their own assignments and student work from their own classes and received feedback from colleagues. Writing became a focus for professional development at Park East. Reflecting on the positive feedback they gathered from the professional development sessions, the committee members continued to identify ways to incorporate looking together at student work into the school's professional development. As one teacher reflected,

> Even though we've done this many times before, every time we do one of these, I am impressed by how useful they [the protocols] are. Today . . . I saw what was possible in terms of high-quality student writing and learned about a new way to get them there. Pretty good.

CHAPTER 6

Facilitating Protocols

FACILITATING PROTOCOLS IS BOTH straightforward and complex. The basics are simple: Convene a group, introduce the protocol, and then move the group step by step through it. But, like most useful skills, good facilitation requires practice. With practice comes the capacity to address a whole range of challenges that can emerge when using protocols. These include knowing which protocol(s) will best match the group's purposes, helping group members to refocus when they stray from the topic, encouraging group members to delve more deeply and productively into the work being presented, supporting a presenter who becomes defensive or unfocused, and so on.

In this chapter, we share a few basics to help novice facilitators get started in facilitating protocols like those described in Chapters 4 and 5. For a more extended discussion of facilitation skills and challenges, see *The Facilitator's Book of Questions* (Allen & Blythe, 2004) and other publications in the List of Resources.

HOW FACILITATORS THINK

Facilitating a protocol resembles two other kinds of facilitation roles that teachers and administrators are usually familiar with: leading a workshop or training session and running a meeting or a committee. In all three cases, the facilitator has particular responsibility for guiding the efforts of the group. But two key differences shape the mindset of a protocol facilitator, making the things he or she pays attention to significantly different from those attended to by workshop leaders or meeting facilitators.

Supporting Learning

Protocol facilitators seek primarily to support the learning of the individual participants and the group as a whole. In this respect, their role differs from that of the meeting facilitator. The leader of a faculty meeting or a committee is usually charged with making sure the group accomplishes something concrete—that they complete a certain set of tasks, solve a certain set of problems, cover specific information, or develop an action plan. While all these things may happen in the course of a protocol for looking at student work, they are not the primary purpose for protocols. A protocol, with its carefully delineated steps, is designed to be a learning experience for both the presenter and the group members. Protocol facilitators regularly ask themselves, "How is this protocol supporting the learning of the participants?"

Focusing on Process

The protocol facilitator focuses on the group's collaboration rather than the topic of the discussion. This is the quality that distinguishes the protocol facilitator from a workshop leader. Workshop leaders typically have expertise in a particular content, for example, instructional technique. Their job is to share that expertise with the participants, helping them to develop their own expertise in that area.

By contrast, protocol facilitators focus on the group's process to ensure that the group follows the steps of the protocol; however, they do not seek to contribute their own content expertise. In protocols, such expertise is brought by the group members themselves. The protocol becomes the vehicle for sharing this expertise. The facilitator's job is to ensure that the expertise is shared among the group—not to provide it him- or herself. Workshop leaders might ask themselves, "Are the group members understanding the essential points of this topic?" By contrast, protocol facilitators ask themselves, "Does everyone understand the protocol? Are we using it productively? Is the protocol affording all participants the chance to share their expertise and learn from one another?"

WHAT FACILITATORS DO

Facilitators of protocols have several specific tasks to carry out. We divide them here into the steps one takes before a protocol, during the protocol, and then after the protocol is over. We address these strategies and tips directly to those who play—or might play—the role of facilitator.

Before the Protocol

The facilitator has some tasks that need to be completed before the meeting even convenes and some that are carried out in the meeting just before beginning the protocol.

Meet with the Presenter. Some time before the group convenes, set up a time to talk with the presenter. In this conversation, you can review the protocol, discuss the presenter's role in it, review the student work he or she would like to bring, and help him or her frame a focusing question (if the protocol asks the presenter to share one). You might ask the presenter, "What do you hope to learn from the protocol experience?"

Set Norms with the Group. Once the group has convened, but before beginning the protocol, spend a few minutes with the participants developing norms (or reminding them of previously developed norms). Norms are the guidelines to which everyone agrees to adhere in order to ensure a respectful and productive discussion. (Some protocols such as the Tuning Protocol have already-established norms or guidelines that the group can use; see Chapter 4.) As the facilitator, you might encourage the group members to identify norms that make explicit the need for respect and sensitivity in their comments—and then to model these norms in your own interactions throughout the session.

Review the Purpose and Steps of the Protocol. It's a good idea to have copies of the protocol so that everyone can track its progress during the meeting. Before beginning the protocol, remind the group of the protocol's purpose and review the steps aloud. Check to see if anyone has questions before you begin, and let the group know it is fine to ask questions about the protocol at any point in the process.

Ask Someone to Document the Group's Conversation. If your group will be meeting regularly, ask someone to take brief notes about the substance of the conversation, important questions that emerge, and any ideas the group has for how to move forward. These notes, however brief, can be an important source of evidence for the group about how its learning is developing over time. As a group, you may want to spend some time in a meeting figuring out how you want to document the group's work and how the documentation notes and other artifacts (including copies of the work presented in the protocols) will be saved.

During the Protocol

Once the protocol has begun, the facilitator maintains his or her focus on guiding the process of the group and supporting the quality of their learning experience. The facilitator typically uses several specific strategies to do this.

Move the Group Through the Steps of the Protocol. The facilitator introduces each step of the protocol. Discussing student work is a very thought-provoking process. It raises diverse and complex issues for the people involved in it. In order to keep the discussion focused, you may need to provide reminders about the topic or question that is currently on the table or about the time limit for a given portion of the schedule. Some facilitators invite everyone to share the responsibility for keeping the conversation on track.

Try Not to Participate in the Substance of the Conversation. It is very easy to get caught up in a discussion and, as a result, lose track of facilitation responsibilities, such as making sure everyone has a chance to speak and sticking to agreed-upon time limits. Although it is not impossible for one person to act as both facilitator and participant, it is probably not a good starting place for a novice facilitator. If no one in the group wants to give up the chance to be an active participant ("talker") in the conversation, you might consider inviting a person from outside the group to facilitate the meeting.

Maintain a Nonjudgmental Attitude. The success of any process for looking at student work is dependent on the group members' ability to share their thoughts honestly and respectfully. Criticism from you about participants' comments or about the presenter's work will prevent a conversation of any depth from developing. Even comments that imply a positive assessment ("Excellent point!") are, nonetheless, judgments and can have a similar effect. By contrast, respectfully accepting all contributions (that are appropriate for the protocol) may encourage people to speak honestly. For instance, responding to an ambiguous comment with "Could you explain a little more about what you mean?" is more helpful than "That's confusing" or "That's off the topic." "Respectful acceptance" does not mean that you have to sit by idly while the comments wander further and further away from the agenda, but rather that care should be used in redirecting participants to the agreed-upon topic or schedule.

Encourage Evidence-Based Conversation. Discussions using protocols become more powerful and useful to presenters and participants when the discussion is evidence based. A facilitator can encourage evidence-based conversations by asking participants to be concrete and specific in their comments and questions. For example, after a participant offers feedback, you might ask him or her to point to the place(s) in the student work that led to that comment. A simple question such as "What makes you say that?" can make a significant difference in the quality of a participant's question or comment.

After the Protocol

To continue to support the learning of the group, the presenter, and themselves, facilitators usually take several other steps at the conclusion of a protocol.

Talk with the Group About Next Steps. Once the group has completed the debriefing of the protocol (usually the last step in a protocol), the facilitator officially closes the protocol, thanks the presenter, and then asks the group about next steps: "When do you want to meet next? Who will present student work? What protocol feels like it might be a good fit for our group's purposes?"

Check in with the Presenter. Sometime after the meeting has adjourned, many protocol facilitators check in with the presenter to see what he or she thought of the conversation. This check-in might take place immediately after the meeting is over or it might occur several days later. The purpose of the check-in is not accountability ("Is he or she putting new ideas into practice?"). Rather, it is recognition of the particular role the presenter is asked to play in a protocol—listening to one's students being discussed by others is a challenging task. Often there is much feedback to take in and digest. While most protocols give the presenter the chance to share his or her reactions out loud with the group at the end of the protocol, it may take additional time for thoughts and reactions to percolate. Your brief check-in with the presenter can ensure that his or her reactions and feedback— especially about the process itself—can help to shape the group's work in the future.

Reflect on Your Own Facilitation Efforts (Without Being Overly Critical). Facilitators make many, many decisions before, during, and after protocols. For example, a facilitator may need to decide when to interrupt a conversation that is heating up but that may not be relevant to the presenter's focusing question or the group's goals. All facilitators—even very experienced ones—make poor calls from time to time, such as intervening when staying out of the conversation might have been better, or failing to intervene when a well-chosen word or question might have helped to reorient the group. When a misstep seems to be interfering with the progress of the conversation, it is usually possible to call a "facilitator's time out" and talk with the group about the best way to continue the protocol. But even if you didn't take steps in the meeting to correct the course of the conversation, reflecting on your own facilitation afterward, individually or with others from your group, can help you develop your skills. Remember: Like teaching, facilitation is as much art as science!

List of Resources

PUBLICATIONS AND VIDEOS

Looking Collaboratively at Student Work (General)

Allen, D. (Ed.). (1998). *Assessing student learning: From grading to understanding.* New York: Teachers College Press.

Allen, D., & Blythe T. (2004). *The facilitator's book of questions: Tools for looking together at student and teacher work.* New York: Teachers College Press.

Annenberg Institute for School Reform. (1999). *Looking at student work: A window into the classroom* [Video]. New York: Teachers College Press.

Bella, N. J. (2004). *Reflective analysis of student work: Improving teaching through collaboration.* Thousand Oaks, CA: Corwin Press.

Cushman, K. (1996). Looking collaboratively at student work: An essential toolkit [Whole issue]. *Horace, 13*(2). Available from Coalition of Essential Schools.

Evidence Project Staff at Project Zero, Harvard Graduate School of Education. (2001). *The evidence process: A collaborative approach to understanding and improving teaching and learning.* Cambridge, MA: Author. Available from Harvard Project Zero.

Little, J. W., Gearhart, M., Curry, M., & Kafka, J. (2003). Looking at student work for teacher learning, teacher community, and school reform. *Phi Delta Kappan, 85*(3), 185–192.

McDonald, J., Mohr, N., Dichter, A., & McDonald, E. (2003). *The power of protocols: An educator's guide to better practice.* New York: Teachers College Press.

Weinbaum, A., Allen, D., Blythe, T., Simon, K., Seidel, S., & Rubin, C. (2004). *Teaching as inquiry: Asking hard questions to improve practice and student achievement.* New York: Teachers College Press.

The Tuning Protocol

Allen, D. (1998). The Tuning Protocol: Opening up reflection. In D. Allen (Ed.), *Assessing student learning: From grading to understanding* (pp. 87–104). New York: Teachers College Press.

McDonald, J. P., Smith, S., Turner, D., Finney, M., & Barton, E. (1993). *Graduation by exhibition: Assessing genuine achievement.* Alexandria, VA: Association for Supervision and Curriculum Development.

The Collaborative Assessment Conference

Seidel, S. (1998a). Learning from looking. In N. Lyons (Ed.), *With portfolio in hand: Validating the new teacher professionalism* (pp. 69–89). New York: Teachers College Press.

Seidel, S. (1998b). Wondering to be done: The collaborative assessment conference. In D. Allen (Ed.), *Assessing student learning: From grading to understanding* (pp. 21–39). New York: Teachers College Press.

The Consultancy

Carr, J. F., Herman, N., & Harris, D. E. (2005). *Creating dynamic schools through mentoring, coaching, and collaboration.* Alexandria, VA: Association for Supervision and Curriculum Development.

Nolan, J., Jr., & Hoover, L. A. (2005). *Teacher supervision and evaluation: Theory into practice (update edition).* Hoboken, NJ: Wiley.

Descriptive Review Processes

Featherstone, H. (1998). Studying children: The Philadelphia Teachers' Learning Cooperative. In D. Allen (Ed.), *Assessing student learning: From grading to understanding* (pp. 66–83). New York: Teachers College Press.

Himley, M. (Ed.), with Carini, P. (2000). *From another angle: Children's strengths and school standards: The Prospect Center's descriptive review of the child.* New York: Teachers College Press.

School Improvement

McDonald, J. P. (1996). *Redesigning school: Lessons for the 21st Century.* San Francisco: Jossey-Bass.

Neufeld, B., & Woodworth, K. (2000). *Taking stock: The status of implementation and the needs for further support in the BPE CAC Cohort I and II schools.* Boston: Education Matters, Inc. http://www.edmatters.org/reports.html

Newmann, F., & Associates (1996). *Authentic achievement: Restructuring schools for intellectual quality.* San Francisco: Jossey-Bass.

Sebring, P. B., Allensworth, E., Bryk, A. S., Easton, J. Q., & Luppescu, S. (2006). *The essential supports for school improvement.* Chicago: Consortium on Chicago School Research at the University of Chicago. http://ccsr.uchicago.edu/publications/EssentialSupports.pdf

Projects

Berger, R. (1996). *A culture of quality: A reflection on practice.* Providence, RI: Annenberg Institute for School Reform. Available from the Annenberg Institute for School Reform.

Levy, S. (1996). *Engaging children's minds: The project approach.* Norwood, NJ: Ablex.

Powell, B. S. (1996) *Toward understanding: Observations from two classrooms.* Providence, RI: Annenberg Institute for School Reform. Available from the Annenberg Institute for School Reform.

Wigginton, E., & Students. (1991). *Starting from scratch: One classroom builds its own curriculum.* Portsmouth, NH: Heinemann.

About Portfolios

Jervis, K. (1996). *Eyes on the child: Three portfolio stories.* New York: Teachers College Press.

Lyons, N. (Ed.). (1998). *With portfolio in hand: Validating the new teacher professionalism.* New York: Teachers College Press.

Seidel, S., Walters, J., Kirby, E., Olff, N., Powell, K., Scripp, L., & Veenema, S. (1996). *Portfolio practices: Thinking through the assessment of student work.* Washington, DC: NEA Publications Library. Available from Harvard Project Zero.

Winner, E. (Ed.). (1992). *The Arts PROPEL handbooks* [a general handbook and one each for music, creative writing, and visual arts]. Cambridge, MA: Harvard Project Zero. Available from Harvard Project Zero.

Wolf, D. P. (1989). Portfolio assessment: Sampling student work. *Educational Leadership, 46*(7), 35–39.

Assessment (General)

Carini, P. (2001). *Starting strong: A different look at children, schools, and standards.* New York: Teachers College Press.

Darling-Hammond, L., Ancess, J., & Falk, B. (1995). *Authentic assessment in action: Studies of schools and students at work.* New York: Teachers College Press.

Engel, B. (2005). *Holding values: What we mean by progressive education: Essays by members of the North Dakota Study Group.* Portsmouth, NH: Heinemann Press.

Falk, B. (1998). Looking at students and their work: Supporting diverse learners with the Primary Language Record. In D. Allen (Ed.), *Assessing student learning: From grading to understanding* (pp. 40–65). New York: Teachers College Press.

Falk, B. (2000). *The heart of the matter: Using standards and assessment to learn.* Portsmouth, NH: Heinemann.

Herman, J. L., Aschbacher, P. R., & Winters, L. (1992). *A practical guide to alternative assessment.* Alexandria, VA: Association for Supervision and Curriculum Development.

Mitchell, R. (1992). *Testing for learning: How new approaches to evaluation can improve American schools.* New York: Free Press.

Newmann, F., Secada, W., & Wehlage, G. (1995). *A guide to authentic instruction and assessment: Vision, standards, and scoring.* Madison, WI: Wisconsin Center for Educational Research.

Pellegrino, J. W., Chudowsky, N., & Glaser, R. (Eds.). (2001). *Knowing what stu-*

dents know: The science and design of educational assessment. Washington, DC: National Academy Press.

Perrone, V. (1991). *Expanding student assessment.* Alexandria, VA: Association for Supervision and Curriculum Development.

Stiggins, R. J. (2001). *Student-involved classroom assessment.* Upper Saddle River, NJ: Merrill Prentice Hall.

Wiggins, G.P. (1998). *Educative assessment: Designing assessments to inform and improve student performance.* San Francisco: Jossey-Bass.

Facilitating Groups

Allen, D., & Blythe T. (2004). *The facilitator's book of questions: Tools for looking together at student and teacher work.* New York: Teachers College Press.

Kaner, S., Lind, L., Told, C., Fisk, S., & Berger, D. (2007). *Facilitator's guide to participatory decision-making.* San Francisco: Jossey-Bass.

Perkins, D. (2003). *King Arthur's Round Table: How collaborative conversations create smart organizations.* Hoboken, NJ: Wiley.

Schwarz, R. (2002). *The skilled facilitator: A comprehensive resource for consultants, facilitator, managers, trainers, and coaches.* (2nd ed.). San Francisco: Jossey-Bass.

ORGANIZATIONS

Annenberg Institute for School Reform
Brown University (Box 1985)
Providence, RI 02912
(401) 863–7990
http://www.annenberginstitute.org

Coalition of Essential Schools
1814 Franklin Street
Oakland, CA 94612
(510) 433–1451
http://www.essentialschools.org

National Center for Restructuring
 Education, Schools and Teaching
 (NCREST)
Teachers College, Columbia
 University (Box 110)
New York, NY 10027
http://www.tc.edu/ncrest

National School Reform Faculty
Harmony Education Center
PO Box 1787
Bloomington, IN 47402
(812) 330–2702
www.harmonyschool.org/nsrf

Project Zero
Harvard Graduate School of Education
124 Mount Auburn Street, 5th Floor
Cambridge, MA 02138
(617) 495–4342
http://pzweb.harvard.edu

The Prospect Center
PO Box 328
North Bennington, VT 05257
www.prospectcenter.org

About the Authors

TINA BLYTHE is a middle school social studies teacher, adjunct lecturer at the Harvard Graduate School of Education, and director of faculty development at the Boston Architectural College. As a consultant she works with schools, districts, and organizations both nationally and internationally. For 16 years she was a researcher at Harvard Project Zero. Her work has focused on multiple intelligences, instructional approaches that foster complex thinking and understanding, authentic assessment, and professional development for educators (particularly teachers' collaborative inquiry). Her most recent books are *The Facilitator's Book of Questions: Tools for Looking at Student and Teacher Work* (with David Allen, 2004) and *Teaching as Inquiry: Asking Hard Questions to Improve Practice and Student Achievement* (Weinbaum et al., 2004).

DAVID ALLEN is a senior research associate at the National Center for Restructuring Education, Schools, and Teaching (NCREST) at Teachers College, Columbia University. He has also worked at Project Zero at the Harvard Graduate School of Education and the Coalition of Essential Schools, then at Brown University. His work has focused on authentic assessment, teachers' collaborative inquiry, school coaching, and small schools. He has taught English and ESL in middle school, high school, college, and adult education settings. He received a Fulbright grant to study school reform in Poland. His most recent books are *The Facilitator's Book of Questions: Tools for Looking at Student and Teacher Work* (with Tina Blythe, 2004) and *Teaching as Inquiry: Asking Hard Questions to Improve Practice and Student Achievement* (Weinbaum et al., 2004).

BARBARA SCHIEFFELIN POWELL, an educational consultant, is currently project director of Exploring Humanitarian Law, a worldwide curriculum for youth 13–18 designed by the Education Development Center and the International Committee of the Red Cross. As a researcher she has studied high school change for the Coalition of Essential Schools, then at Brown University; evaluated Teach for America's summer training institute; and assessed the impact of the arts on students. Previously she taught secondary school English and history in Malawi and in the United States. She has been a high school principal and has taught at Wellesley College; Harvard University; and the University of Bielefeld, Germany. Her current interests focus on international curriculum development, teacher training, and evaluation.